THE
WATER GARDEN
ENCYCLOPEDIA

THE
WATER GARDEN
ENCYCLOPEDIA

Philip Swindells

FIREFLY BOOKS

A FIREFLY BOOK

Published by Firefly Books Ltd., 2003

First Printing

National Library of Canada Cataloguing in Publication Data
Swindells, Philip
        The water garden encyclopedia / Philip Swindells.
Includes index.
ISBN 1-55297-715-3 (bound).—ISBN 1-55297-717-X (pbk.)
        1. Water gardens. I. Title.
SB423.S944 2003   635.9'674   C2002-904101-5

U.S. Cataloging in Publication Data
(Library of Congress Standards)

Swindells, Philip.
     The water garden encyclopedia / Philip Swindells. – 1st ed.
[256] p. : col. ill. , photos. ; cm.
Includes index.
Summary: A comprehensive guide to designing, building and maintaining residential water gardens.
ISBN 1-55297-715-3
ISBN 1-55297-717-X (pbk.)
1. Water gardens. I. Title.
635.9/ 674 21   SB423.S938 2003

Published in Canada in 2003 by
Firefly Books Ltd.
3680 Victoria Park Avenue
Toronto, Ontario M2H 3K1

Published in the United States in 2003
by Firefly Books (U.S.) Inc.
P.O. Box 1338, Ellicott Station
Buffalo, New York 14205

Editor: Philip de Ste. Croix
Designer: Philip Clucas MSIAD
Studio photography: Neil Sutherland
Artwork: Rod Ferring, Martin Reed, John Sutton and Stuart Watkinson
Production management: Consortium, Poslingford, Suffolk, England
Print production: Leefung-Asco Printers Ltd., China
Printed and bound in China

Acknowledgments:
The publishers would like to thank the following people for their help during the preparation of this book: Anthony Archer-Wills and Gail Paterson at New Barn Aquatic Nurseries, West Chiltington; Mike and Wendy Yendell of Aristaquatics, Billinghurst; Old Barn Nurseries, Dial Post, Horsham; Graham and Howard Healey at Four Seasons Bonsai Nursery, East Peckham; Hillbour Ltd.; Stephen Markham; Stuart Thraves at Blagdon, Bridgwater; Murrells Nursery, Pullborough; Graham Quick; Geoff Rogers; Stonessscapes, Cranleigh; and Bulldog Tools.

contents

introduction

Water gardening is one of the most exciting styles of gardening. Within a pool there exists a complete underwater world where plants, fish, snails and other creatures depend upon one another for their continued existence. Managing such a complex world successfully is enormously satisfying.

Not that the water garden is solely the pool, for there can be spreading margins and bog areas which offer great opportunities for growing a rich diversity of plants that cannot otherwise be cultivated in the garden. Where garden space is restricted, then plants and fish can be enjoyed equally well in tubs and containers.

Most people appreciate the great beauty of waterlilies, the most exotic of all aquatics which are available in varieties from the pygmies that will dwell in a couple of inches of water to giants with blossoms the size of soup dishes which must be grown in a lake. Deep-water aquatics are suitable companion plants that are useful for smaller bodies of water where their spread does not dominate. Marginal aquatics and bog garden plants dress the poolside with character and color, while submerged aquatics and free-floating plants provide the necessary requirements to ensure a balanced eco-system.

Ornamental fish add life and movement to the water. Available in a wide array of shapes, sizes and colors there are many hardy varieties that will co-exist and often breed successfully in the garden pond. Snails and freshwater

mussels complete the picture as far as the requirements for creating a balanced environment are concerned, but frogs, toads and newts often choose to make their home in a water garden and they are an added bonus.

Water is an attraction in its own right. Such a feature need not be dressed with plants in order to be visually appealing or successful. Moving water, whether fountain, waterfall or stream, holds an attraction of its own, and with the addition of lighting the effect can become magical. While tumbling waterfalls and cascading fountains are traditional and much-loved features of the water garden, pleasing moving water creations can be achieved on a smaller scale with bubblers and millstones.

Ornaments and decorative features of all kinds can be introduced to a water garden–not only spouting statuary, but islands, bridges and causeways. The opportunities for creating an outstanding garden feature are legion. A pool may be at its peak of perfection during summer but it also has great attributes at other times of the year, even during winter. It is in winter that the water can be seen at its best, devoid of foliage–a beautiful natural mirror reflecting all about it. A water garden is truly an all-year-round attraction and irrespective of its scale provides great pleasure. It can be as complex or as simple as desired, and with the modern materials that are now available the creation of an attractive water feature should be within the capabilities of all.

Above: *An attractive wall fountain that would grace any small garden.*
Right: *This statue of a crane, situated on an island surrounded by calm water and seen against a backdrop of flowering wisteria, epitomizes the magic of water gardening.*

getting started

It is not difficult to get started with a water garden. The problem more often lies in the rich diversity of choices that are available and deciding upon the right one for you. Most garden centers offer a wide range of ponds, pumps, filters, lights and ornaments to suit all pockets. When making a decision it is best to choose the most robust and the highest quality that can be afforded within your budget.

Do not be in a great hurry to buy all the equipment at once. Decide upon what is ultimately desirable and then buy as finances allow. Each major item can be installed separately, provided that any necessary provisions for cables and such are made from the outset. Careful planning is the most important aspect of making a successful start.

With ponds there are several construction options, but requirements usually dictate the materials used. Specially shaped ponds normally require a liner, natural features either a liner or a bentonite blanket, while patio and small formal arrangements benefit from a preformed structure.

Most modern pumps are submersible, but there are occasions when a traditional surface pump and chamber are useful. Nowadays submersible pumps are available for tiny indoor water features where they can be hidden in the base of a pot, as well as for producing substantial fountains and waterfalls in large outdoor pools.

Filters are available in a range of sizes and types. Often it is useful to establish the pond and assess what the requirements are for the filter before making a decision. Similarly with lighting, it is often best to get the plants established before coming to a conclusion as to what should be lit and how best this can be achieved.

Even small water features can bring liquid sound and movement to an otherwise dull corner of a garden.

basic principles

When establishing a water garden it is important to take into account a number of considerations, the most critical one being siting. Ideally a garden pool, or other water feature where plants are to figure prominently, should be constructed in a position of full and uninterrupted sunlight. For a viable eco-system to be established, lusty plant growth is essential and all aquatic plants must have plenty of light.

Visually water is always more appealing when situated at the lowest point in the landscape. This cannot always be arranged, but when it can, take care to see that the site is not waterlogged and that the water table does not rise dramatically during the winter. A water table close to the surface of the soil can cause unwanted ballooning of a pool liner, the pressure of ground water outside forcing the liner away from the poolside or even displacing a preformed pool up out of the ground.

It is also essential to know where services to the house or other buildings are laid. It is extremely frustrating to be close to completing an excavation and coming unexpectedly across a water or gas main. Conversely if water or an electrical supply is to be laid within easy reach of the water garden, provisions for their installation must be made before pond construction begins.

Any use of electricity should strictly comply with regulations, and all equipment must be specifically manufactured for use with water. Nowadays there are a wide range of pumps, lights and other electrical equipment available which comply with strict codes of practice. This is a very important consideration for the gardener as well as his or her children, for water features are dangerous places for play and suitable precautions should be employed to prevent accidents. Where young children are likely to play in the garden, it may be necessary to fence off the pool or cover it with sturdy wire netting until they have reached an age at which an accidental fall into the pool will not pose a potentially life-threatening danger.

FACTS AND FIGURES

- One US gallon of water occupies 231 cubic inches.
- One US gallon is equivalent to 0.833 imperial gallons and weighs 8.3 lbs.
- One cubic foot of water is equivalent to 7.49 US gallons and weighs 62.32 lbs.
- One quart equals 2 pints or 32 fluid ounces.
- One liter equals 1.057 liquid quarts.

Above and right: *These are not good sites for a pool. A low area, which collects water, can cause problems during the winter, the pressure of ground water ballooning a pool liner or lifting a preformed pool. Tree roots can cause similar problems, and shade and fallen leaves are undesirable.*

CALCULATING POOL CAPACITY

It is relatively easy to calculate the capacity of regularly shaped pools. You measure the surface area of the pool (length x width) and multiply this figure by the average depth to come to a figure for volume.

Irregular pools are harder to assess. The best method is to draw the outline shape of the pool accurately on graph paper. You should then count up the number of squares occupied by the pool's surface to enable you to calculate the surface area. Squares that are only partially occupied should be added together to reach the total. It is not 100 per cent accurate, but it does give a good indication. This figure is then multiplied by the average depth to arrive at the cubic volume.

WARNING Electricity and water make a dangerous combination. Ensure that any electrical device running off mains power is protected by a residual current device (RCD) or circuit breaker which will cut off the supply instantly in the event of a short-circuit. All external connections should be weatherproof. All cables should be buried underground in deep trenches and ideally protected by a layer of slabs or tiles positioned above the cable to prevent it being accidentally severed by anyone unwittingly digging in the area.

Below: *This pond illustrates the problems of building on a slope. Because levels were not properly checked during excavation, the pool is not level. The liner is exposed on the right while water laps the rim on the left.*

Right: *Underground pipes and cables can create difficulties during pool construction, especially when they are come upon during excavation. Check where pipes run while planning the pool.*

CHECKLIST

- Situate the water feature in full sun.
- Keep away from overhanging trees because of falling leaves and disruptive roots.
- Keep away from trees of the cherry family, the winter host of the waterlily aphid.
- Check the location of existing underground services to avoid damaging them during excavation.
- Prepare the site for installation of required underground services, e.g. electricity.
- Visually water is best placed at the lowest point in the landscape, but avoid waterlogged areas.
- Ensure that the site does not flood. Install a drain if necessary.
- Ensure the provision of suitable depths of water for both deep-water and marginal aquatics.
- Make any preparations necessary to ensure that safety measures can be made to keep children safe.

options and materials

There are many different methods available for constructing water features. No longer are puddled clay or concrete the main materials for producing a waterproof lining. A wide array of synthetic linings from pvc and polyethylene to rubber and bentonite matting have revolutionized pond construction. Preformed ponds of fiberglass, plastic or composition materials offer another simple method of creating a water garden, although these do not give quite the flexibility of design allowed by pond liners.

Pond liners are used to line an excavation that is the shape of the final pond. In many cases pond liners are vulnerable to damage, especially in stony soil, and so an underlay has to be provided. This is usually in the form of a specially manufactured material, although household products such as thick wads of dampened newspaper or discarded carpet are often utilized.

Streams are most effectively created with a liner, for they can be more imaginatively designed and the levels better controlled than by the use of preformed sections that clip together. Twists and turns in the stream bed are also more easily accommodated with a flexible liner.

The same applies with waterfall and cascade units. When preformed they have the advantage of being watertight, quick to use and producing a consistent spread and flow of water, but the materials from which they are made often have a rather artificial appearance. They are not as easy to make look convincing in a natural setting as a liner dressed with well-placed rocks and softened by planted edges.

MAKING PREPARATIONS

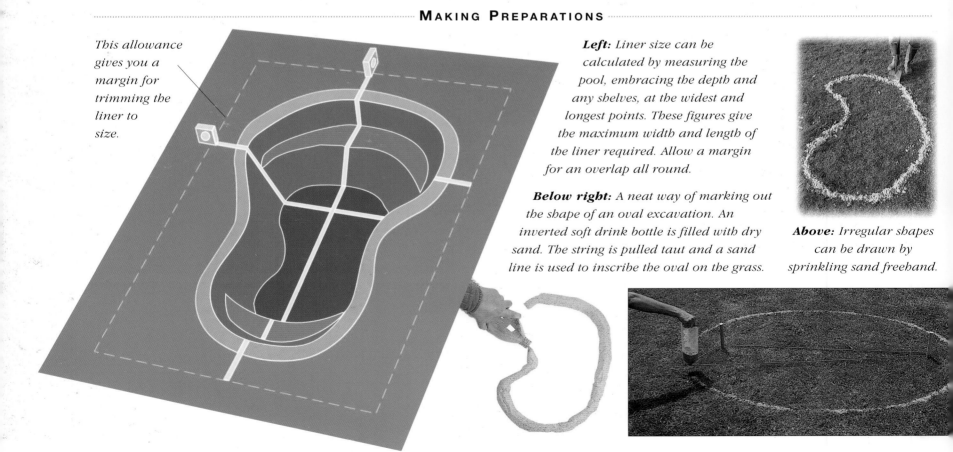

This allowance gives you a margin for trimming the liner to size.

Left: *Liner size can be calculated by measuring the pool, embracing the depth and any shelves, at the widest and longest points. These figures give the maximum width and length of the liner required. Allow a margin for an overlap all round.*

Below right: *A neat way of marking out the shape of an oval excavation. An inverted soft drink bottle is filled with dry sand. The string is pulled taut and a sand line is used to inscribe the oval on the grass.*

Above: *Irregular shapes can be drawn by sprinkling sand freehand.*

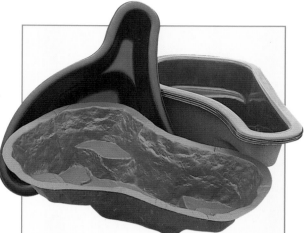

Above: *There are a wide variety of preformed pools available in a selection of materials. All are very durable and not difficult to install. Make sure that the marginal shelves are sufficiently large to accommodate planting baskets.*

Above: *Preformed cascade units are easily installed and rarely present any problems with water seepage around the edges. However, they are more difficult to disguise with planting than liner.*

Right: *Preformed cascade units are ideal for small water features. With larger arrangements, the use of a liner and rocks is more desirable. A waterfall using a liner is quite demanding to build if there is to be no water seepage. The arrangement of the levels and the placement of rocks also require care if the outcome is to look natural.*

adding other elements

The gardener who wishes to extend a water feature, perhaps by creating a waterfall or fountain, has many options. It is not necessary to put together a complex proposal, for at the garden center many exciting options await the enthusiast. Preformed waterfalls and cascade units take much of the work out of creating such a feature. Not only are they guaranteed to be watertight, but they are of such a configuration that when the pump is switched off, some water remains lying in the units.

Pumps are often included as part of a package, and sometimes, as with a wall fountain, are built into the structure. There are very elaborate kits around where it is not necessary to know anything about the pump, other than that it is attached and will function adequately if connected to the electrical supply. This is particularly

evident with wooden tubs and traditional village pump arrangements.

There are a whole range of ready-made fountains which comprise an ornament and a pump that just need placing in the pool and switching on. Some are tiny and can be used in pot or container arrangements, while others are gushing jets in the best traditions of classical designs and require a generous spread of water.

Modern interchangeable hoses, connectors, valves and couplings all provide instant watertight connections which enable the water gardener to put together innovative designs if the package or kit is not appealing. No longer are soldering and brazing essential skills for constructing exciting and unusual creations. A spanner and screwdriver are usually all that is required.

HOSES, CONNECTORS, TAPS AND COUPLINGS

This page: *There are a wide range of pipes and easily installed pipe fittings available off the shelf at the garden center or DIY store. These make the production of quite elaborate arrangements simple, even for the beginner. The most versatile and durable pipe is ridged like a vacuum cleaner hose.*

Right: *A waterfall can be an absolute joy when illuminated in the evening. Here all the elements of moving water, pool and plants have come together and are enhanced by carefully placed lights. These are easy to install and not expensive to maintain. They add a new dimension to the garden.*

Left: *A pool liner is a good option for creating a waterfall or stream. Special felt underlay is used to cushion and protect the liner from any protruding sharp stones in the soil.*

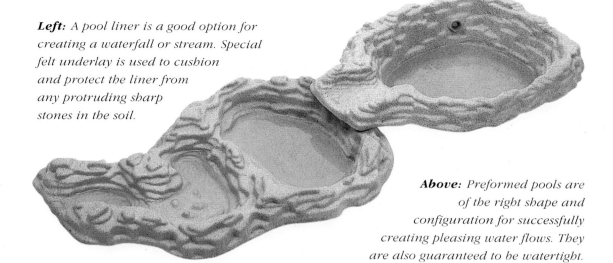

Above: *Preformed pools are of the right shape and configuration for successfully creating pleasing water flows. They are also guaranteed to be watertight.*

pumps and filters

There are two main kinds of pumps: submersible and surface. For most gardeners the surface kinds are now of little relevance for they are only employed to displace very large volumes of water and are rarely necessary in a home situation. Apart from their scale, surface pumps demand a specially constructed brick chamber and often very elaborate pipework, which is mostly beyond the capabilities of the average gardener.

Above: This pump does not move water but it distributes air into the water and is intended as a means of oxygenating a pool where there is a large population of fish.

The component parts of a modern submersible pump showing the power unit, impeller, impeller housing, fountain jet with dual output to both fountain head and waterfall, filter foam and the filter strainer.

With a pump the most important factor is the flow rate: the amount of water that the pump displaces per minute or hour and the effect that has upon the feature. A simple test to calculate the necessary capacity involves measuring the desired water flow for one minute, converting it into gallons or quarts and multiplying the figure by 60 to give a flow rate per hour.

Submersible pumps are available in wide variety and can fulfill most of the requirements of the average pond owner. Even quite compact units can thrust a significant jet of water into the air and at the same time produce a pleasing waterfall. There are also miniature pumps which can conversely yield a modest flow compatible with the tiniest container feature.

Filters are also useful adjuncts to a pump, especially in a pool where there is no prospect of natural balance, as is usually the case where moving water dominates. There are three main filtration systems. The mechanical kind physically removes debris and suspended particles by passing water through a filter medium. Biological filters depend on the action of bacteria to digest waste products in the water (see also page 242), while UV filters use ultraviolet light to kill algae and other micro-organisms.

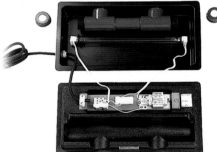

Left: The ultraviolet filter is effective against all algae. Water that is laden with suspended algae returns to the pond clear. UV filtration is the most reliable method of ensuring clear water where a natural balance is impossible to establish.

Right: Before purchasing a pump it is important to ensure that the water flow rate is right. The figure can be established by running a hosepipe into a cascade unit or bucket at a rate that satisfies you and measuring the water flowing over it for the period of a minute.

TAKING A PUMP APART

1 *Submersible pumps are constructed in simple sections which pull apart. In order to get into the pump, it is essential first to remove the shroud which covers the filter foam.*

2 *Once the shroud or strainer has been separated, the filter foam is revealed. It is periodically necessary to remove this for cleaning.*

3 *In order to clean the pump thoroughly, it is necessary to remove the impeller, which lies behind a casing like this. It is located in the part of the pump with the motor. It is this which moves the water.*

4 *Gently remove the impeller with a firm tug. It contains a powerful magnet and requires a stronger pull than may at first be appreciated.*

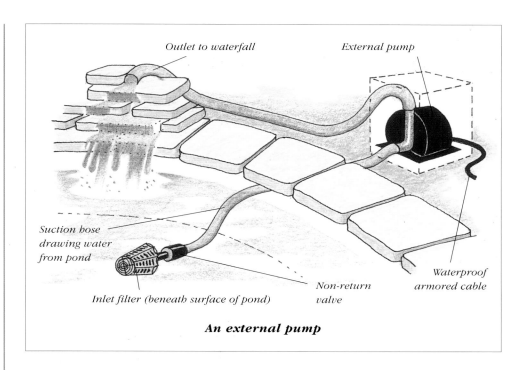

Outlet to waterfall   External pump

Suction hose drawing water from pond

Inlet filter (beneath surface of pond)

Non-return valve

Waterproof armored cable

An external pump

Left: *This is a multi-brush filter unit. The filter brushes take out most of the suspended material. The additional filter medium then works both mechanically and biologically. Colonies of bacteria grow on the medium and they convert fish waste into harmless by-products.*

Right: *A compact filter which may be used both in and out of a pool. It operates using a ceramic filter medium. This is placed in the bottom and a thick filter sponge is added. The lid and outlet pipe are then attached. Filters like this help to maintain water clarity.*

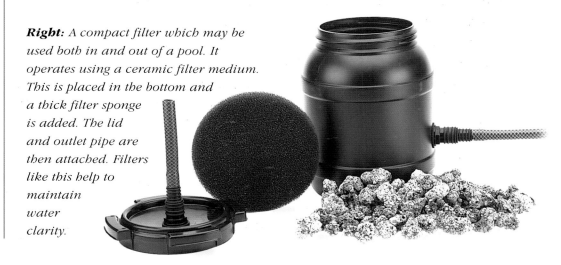

basic design and construction

While it is relatively simple with modern equipment to create a water feature of some kind, it is important to ensure that even with completely self-contained features, basic principles are respected. Even where there are no plants involved, positioning of the feature is critical, both practically and aesthetically.

Water features that include plants must have full light in order that the plants prosper, but where water alone is involved, then it is equally desirable that it should be well lit, for there is little more magical in the garden than the glint of sunlight on a falling curtain of water. The position should also be sheltered from the wind, since the fall of a fountain can be disrupted and the effect ruined if sited on a breezy corner. Not only is this aesthetically undesirable, but splashing water on path or patio is not pleasing either.

Otherwise a water feature can be sited almost anywhere provided that the advice given on pages 10-11 on desirable and undesirable locations has been followed. However, if

Above: *When considering the placement of a water feature, it is important to mark out the area taking into account local features such as the shade cast by trees and incline.*

LAYING AN ELECTRIC CABLE

1 *It is important when laying an electrical cable to a water feature to ensure that it is covered adequately with soil in a deep trench, and that it is manufactured for outdoor use. An armored cable (left) is to be preferred.*

2 *To protect a buried cable from accidental excavation damage, cover it with a layer of sand and lay a course of tiles across the top. The chances of the cable being disturbed by a thrusting spade are remote.*

3 *Once the tiles are securely installed, stick a hazard tape on them. These tapes are weather- and rot-proof and give an early warning of impending danger if digging or other earthmoving activities take place in the immediate vicinity.*

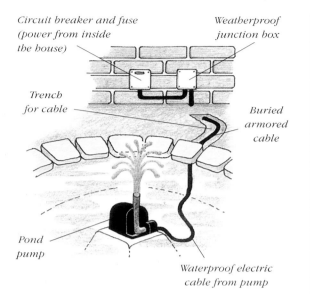

Circuit breaker and fuse
(power from inside
the house)

Weatherproof
junction box

Trench
for cable

Buried
armored
cable

Pond
pump

Waterproof electric
cable from pump

Electrical wiring to the pond

Right: *A pleasing well-balanced pool with accompanying waterfall. This demonstrates how, despite its limitations, moving water can be incorporated into the garden without causing any problems to fish or planting.*

Above: *It is important to get the shape of a pool and stream right before the first turf is cut. Mark out the shape on the ground with hose or rope. Check that everything works visually, and also practically with regard to the lay of the land.*

constructing a waterfall it can be both useful and pleasing to the eye to utilize existing landform. You can carefully sculpt and incorporate an artificial mound into the landscape, but natural topography is generally superior.

Safety should also be a high priority, given that young children may be close to open water, and also considering the electricity used to power the pump. The provision of proper waterproof connectors for cables and their safe installation beneath the soil are major considerations. There are other considerations that are as important as the purely visual aspects. For example, a waterfall should be set up so that when the pump is switched off water still remains in the cascade basins. If you build your basins with a forward tilt, the water will drain away and you will be faced with an unsightly dry water course. This is typical of the many small considerations that must be made. They indicate the importance of carefully thinking through the design of a water feature project before starting construction.

water gardening in containers

Nowadays it does not matter whether you have a garden or not. A water feature is available to everyone. Container water gardens of all kinds can be successfully established in small spaces. Even indoors it is possible to have a table-top fountain dressed with miniature aquatics. Container features are especially useful on balconies, patios and in courtyards where space is restricted. They are also recommended for families with young children as they contain little water and so are very safe.

Container water gardens need not reproduce the traditional water garden pool, although attractive representations can be made using dwarf-growing aquatic plants in sinks, tubs or troughs. Most are created to be enjoyed for the water alone, especially moving water in various guises. Colored stones and rocks, as well as ornaments, figure prominently, and timber and bamboo are also important materials, particularly for the more rustic creations.

The do-it-yourself enthusiast has great opportunities for producing an innovative feature, since any container that holds water is a potential water garden. There are no rules as to what can be utilized.

For those who are only moderately practical there are container water garden kits available commercially that merely require assembling and filling with water, while others are complete and ready to go without any attention other than putting a plug in the socket. Plants are not a necessity, but are valuable additions for a container water feature. Indeed, many gardeners forsake moving water and use a collection of attractive containers for growing individual groups of aquatic plants.

Containers bring moving water into gardens of every style.

tubs and barrels

Of all the containers that can be used for creating a water garden, tubs and barrels are the easiest to assimilate into the garden scene. Mostly made of natural materials, they blend in well with traditional plantings and landscape features and give a rustic feel.

Originally the tubs and barrels that were used for decorative purposes in gardens were second-hand and had contained other products. Tubs were usually whole barrels which were cut through close to one of the central metal bands, thereby securing the timbers near the top. Often they were obtained in less than perfect condition, having contained tar, vegetable oil, or if you were fortunate, sherry. Such barrels not only needed thorough cleaning before they could be used as water features, but had to be kept constantly wet to overcome the prospect of timber shrinkage and subsequent leaking.

Below: A barrel can become an integral part of a garden arrangement where other pot- and container-grown plants are associated. Thus the character of the corner can be altered by the adjustment of peripheral planting.

Left: *A tub or barrel garden does not have to accommodate plants or always be of serious intent. The addition of humor to the garden is always welcome and is particularly useful in attracting young people to gardening.*

Above: *A water garden in miniature comprising almost all the components of a conventional pond, all living harmoniously within the confines of a tub. This is a perfect solution for a limited space.*

Nowadays an industry has grown up to manufacture tubs and barrels for gardening. They are constructed in such a way that they do not have to be kept constantly wet to ensure they are watertight, and they are made from unsullied timber. Often tubs and barrels which are sold at the garden center are already conveniently waterproofed inside so that only water plants and fish need to be added.

planted tub with fountain

The tub fountain is a very effective option for those who want a small moving water feature which is safe for children. It is also one of the easiest to create from standard materials purchased at a garden center.

There are a wide range of tubs available, some of the wooden ones having been used previously to contain other materials. These should be regarded with caution as the wood might be impregnated with pollutants, in which case internal lining with a piece of pool liner is essential. However, many garden centers now offer wooden tubs which are manufactured for the garden trade, and often these have been waterproofed as well. Of course, there are also tubs made from other materials, and while plastics may not be the first choice in the garden, they should not be completely overlooked.

The selection of a suitable pump must be carefully addressed, since there should be over-capacity to give you the option of turning the flow down to what is required. Never select a pump that will just fulfill the task and no more. This is a false economy.

Left: *An interesting association of fountain and crowded planting in a well-presented tub.*

MAKING A TUB FOUNTAIN

1 *Select a clean watertight tub. Be sure at the time of purchase that the outflow of the pump can be adjusted sufficiently to ensure that the flow of water provides the desired effect. Place the pump in the center of the tub and make any necessary height adjustments to the fountain head.*

2 *Choose suitable plants and place them in position. Some height adjustment using bricks under the pots may be necessary.*

3 *Place a metal grille insert over the pump and thread the plants through carefully. Make sure it is securely positioned, if necessary stapling it in place.*

4 *Fill the tub to the top with clean, fresh water. You must do this regularly to compensate for water loss through evaporation and splash.*

5 *Switch on the pump and make any adjustments necessary by regulating the flow adjuster control.*

6 *Once everything is functioning and the plant arrangement is satisfactory, carefully place stones over the mesh support to hide it from view and in order to provide a suitable dressing for the planting.*

----- **PLANTING SUGGESTIONS** -----

Plants Used

Juncus effusus 'Spiralis'/summer/marginal

Lysimachia nummularia/summer/marginal

Stipa tenuissima/summer/herbaceous

Alternative Plants

Butomus umbellatus/late summer/marginal

Cyperus longus/summer/marginal

Veronica beccabunga/summer/marginal

Right: *The complete tub fountain. It is ideal for terrace or patio.*

barrel and spout

There are a number of arrangements with barrels and replica hand pumps available from garden centers. These also have a submersible pump included and built into the structure. Unlike tub fountains which require an outside sump through which to circulate water, the barrel and spout circulate between one another. Occasional splashes as well as evaporation cause some water loss, but this is not significant, although to retain the best visual effect it is wise continually to observe the water level and to top it up when necessary.

Visually a barrel and spout combination benefits from the addition of aquatic plants. They make little difference to the ecology of the water body, but frame the structure beautifully if well chosen. There are limits to what can be grown, since the water can be quite turbulent and many aquatic plants, including waterlilies, would suffer badly.

Even the very resilient pondlilies or nuphars would not put up with the turbulence. Floating plants also suffer, so it is principally the more resilient marginals and selected submerged aquatics that can be used.

PLANTING A BARREL AND SPOUT

1 *Connect the submersible pump to the outflow pipe in the tub. This is sometimes already attached as an integral feature of the tub when purchased.*

3 *Position the plants in the tub. For most marginal aquatic plants, the depth of the water will be too great and so you must raise the containers on bricks. With tub culture it is necessary to confine the plants to small containers, so they will require repotting annually.*

Above: *Half barrels with hand pumps are very popular self-contained moving water features. They offer an excellent opportunity for growing marginal plants.*

2 *Fill the tub with clean, fresh water. Switch on the submersible pump and make sure that the flow of water through the pump is satisfactory before adding any plants.*

4 *It is desirable to have a few submerged plants in the tub, but these will not make a major contribution to water clarity.*

5 Although it is not essential to have fish, they are beneficial as they clear up mosquito larvae and other aquatic insect pests.

------ **PLANTING SUGGESTIONS** ------

Plants Used

Alisma plantago-aquatica/summer/marginal
Ceratophyllum demersum/submerged
Houttuynia cordata/summer/marginal
Lysimachia ciliata 'Firecracker'/summer/ marginal

Alternative Plants

Juncus effusus 'Spiralis'/summer/marginal
Veronica beccabunga/summer/marginal
Myosotis scorpioides/summer/marginal
Pontederia cordata/late summer/marginal

Left: *A version of the traditional barrel and spout with a swinging wooden pail.*

sinks and troughs

There are many opportunities for creating interesting contained water features from sinks and troughs. Natural stone sinks and old stone cattle troughs are perfect – they use traditional materials that rest easily in the garden and are complementary to a wide array of plants. They can be transformed into miniature aquatic landscapes by the use of pygmy waterlilies and dwarf rushes, or else planted as a bog feature with plants which demand only wet soil.

Apart from stone sinks and troughs, a wide range of other functional receptacles have been manufactured over the years. When discarded, these containers can almost always be turned into a water garden, whether a white glazed sink

Below: A complete miniature water garden can be created in a traditional stone sink, although with such a small volume of water it is impossible to create a natural sustained ecological balance. The water must be periodically changed.

or galvanized cattle trough. The opportunities for innovation are many.

With the addition of hypertufa a glazed sink can be turned into a replica stone one, and with brightly colored metallic paints a galvanized cattle trough can become a trendy psychedelic water feature. There are shiny metal

Above: *This sink contains plants which depend upon their foliage for interest. Only the iris produces colorful blossoms, although the sedges and rushes have interesting seedheads.*

sinks and stainless steel ones too, perfect for adaptation for the modern minimalist garden with its mirrors and colored glass chips.

dressing a sink with hypertufa

Although it is most desirable to use a real stone sink or trough for growing aquatic plants, the reality is that they are quite scarce and also expensive to buy. With a little time and ingenuity a traditional glazed sink can be used and converted into a replica stone vessel by the use of hypertufa. This is an artificial stone-like material which is based upon a naturally occurring stone called tufa. In reality it does not share the same constituents as tufa but, when well-made, hypertufa can be close to indistinguishable to the naked eye.

Tufa is a porous rock, which in nature is found as a calcareous deposit on the bed of streams or in the vicinity of springs. It is formed underwater and when removed to the garden and dried off, it is used in the cultivation of difficult alpine plants. It is quite a scarce and expensive material, and the original production of hypertufa using sand, cement and peat was intended to produce a cheaper alternative. Indeed it is used to produce tufa-like rocks, but also just as frequently to dress glazed sinks for alpine or miniature water gardening so that they appear as if made of natural stone.

PREPARING A HYPERTUFA SINK

1 *Hypertufa is made from a mixture of sand, peat, cement and water. The sand and cement are in equal parts by volume and the peat twice the quantity by volume.*

2 *An old glazed sink must have its surface roughened up with a cold chisel before an adhesive can be applied and the hypertufa mixture added.*

3 *Apply the hypertufa mixture with a small trowel. When mixing, periodically test the moisture content to ensure that it sticks. If too wet or too dry, it may slip off.*

4 *Cover the floor of the sink with well-washed pea gravel. Not only does this disguise the bottom and the plughole, but it catches much of the fine waterborne natural debris.*

5 *To make sure that the water is absolutely clear and to prevent any disturbance of the gravel, pour the water on to a piece of polyethylene. This disperses the water evenly and smoothly.*

6 *Position the plants carefully in their small containers. The plants should be repotted annually in aquatic planting compost.*

A water garden in miniature for terrace, patio or balcony.

······ PLANTING SUGGESTIONS ······

Plants Used

Cyperus eragrostis/summer/marginal
Houttuynia cordata/summer/marginal
Nymphaea 'Pygmaea Graziella'/summer/marginal

Alternative Plants

Juncus effusus 'Spiralis'/summer/marginal
Myosotis scorpioides/summer/marginal
Nymphaea 'Pygmaea Helvola'/summer/waterlily

Above: *Hypertufa provides an opportunity for the gardener who cannot find or afford a traditional stone trough or sink. It looks good when planted with an arrangement of colorful aquatic plants.*

millstones and bubblers

For the introduction into the garden of moving water around which it is safe for children to be, millstones and bubblers are difficult to surpass. All the delights provided by the sight and sound of moving water can be enjoyed with none of the hazards. There is not even the labor of maintaining a conventional water garden where there are always concerns about algae, fish feeding and submerged weed control. Periodically top up the sump with water to compensate for evaporation and flick the switch to activate the pump. That is all there is to it.

Construction can be cheap and easy or complicated and expensive – you have a choice. Kits of all kinds are available to enable you to do it yourself. The millstones may be of reconstituted stone or fiberglass and the cobbles selected and graded to perfection with everything put together in a kit.

On the other hand it is possible to seek out an old millstone and large stone trough or bowl, essentials of the 19th-century farm or mill. These are expensive, but really show their quality and are deserving of the finest reclaimed landscape materials to accompany them. They can be assembled as a do-it-yourself project, but are generally much better put together by a professional.

Below: An unconventional use for a millstone producing a cascade-like effect. Millstone features are often more sedate.

Above: This millstone-like moving water feature demonstrates beautifully how water and stone can combine together to produce an aquatic 'sculpture.' The effect is so pleasing visually that no plants are required to dress the feature.

Left: A drilled stone provides a simple bubbling feature which brings the sound and magic of moving water to the garden, but none of the inherent dangers to children and little of the work demanded from the traditional water gardener. The attractive cobbles are grouped effectively around the bubbling stone but serve to disguise the reservoir beneath.

setting up a millstone

Millstones are wonderful for making safe moving water features. They were never intended for such indignities, but once positioned over a sump, surrounded by cobblestones and tastefully planted, one could argue that they have achieved an even more elevated status than was originally envisaged for them.

Real millstones that have ground flour are not easy to come by, but nowadays a wide array is commercially available in varying sizes, including those made from reconstituted stone, concrete and fiberglass. The reconstituted stone millstones are generally the more pleasing in appearance and once water has flowed over them for a month or two, they take on a weathered look and start to develop a green algal flush.

The most important visual aspect with a millstone feature is to ensure a sufficient flow of water to produce an even spread across a level stone. This may result from a gentle film produced by a strong silent flow, or a bubbling and tumbling from the center of the stone. Either way it is important that the pump selected for the feature is sufficiently powerful to deliver the quantity of water where it is required in an unfettered flow. The manner in which it appears from the center of the stone can be modified to suit your requirements, providing that the amount of water being delivered by the pump is sufficient in the first place.

Right: *The bubbling millstone provides a most effective focal point in this very traditional garden setting.*

MAKING A MILLSTONE FEATURE

1 *Measure the sump accurately. By using two sticks and a string, the dimensions can be transferred to the ground.*

2 *Remove the turf to slightly more than the exact circumference of the sump and dig down to the required depth.*

3 *Level the sump and then secure and support it with pea gravel back-filled between the sump walls and the ground.*

4 *Position the pump in the center of the sump and arrange the cable so that it does not show, ideally by burying it.*

5 *Place the top on the sump and run the cable through the small hand hole that is let into the lid. Then adjust the pump so that the outlet is central with the hole so that the water will pass through the millstone accurately.*

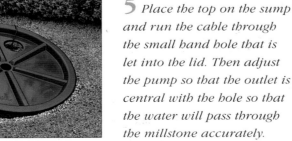

6 *Position the millstone. This is achieved more easily with the use of two pieces of stout timber. It can be slid into position when supported by these, thus reducing the risk of trapped fingers. Fill the sump with water.*

7 *Once the millstone is in position and level, the area above the sump can be decoratively cobbled.*

bubbler in a glazed pot

Not all water features demand plants or fish; indeed the smaller ones are better without them, especially if the water is intended to flow. Such features are very versatile, not only being utilized as features in the garden, but also in the conservatory and occasionally the home as well.

The choice of pots is virtually infinite and most of them can be adapted to use as a fountain water feature. It is the selection of the correct pump that is vital. With most contained water features, the capacity of the pump should be larger than is required to move the volume of water intended, and this holds true for the smaller containers. However, it is conversely also important that the pump can either be turned down, or is sufficiently small that in a confined space it can produce the effect desired rather than dowsing the surrounding area with unwanted water. Nowadays there are some very powerful miniaturized pumps available, so check their flow rates carefully.

Small water features of this nature are essentially for summer enjoyment outdoors; they can be utilized in the conservatory all the year round, but when used in the garden they must be taken indoors as autumn approaches and not set up again outside until late spring when the risk of frosts has passed.

Below: *There are many options for displaying moving water in a ceramic pot. This one uses a specially made series of small saucer-like bowls on a central column.*

MAKING A POT BUBBLER

1 *The pump cable is taken through the drainage hole of the pot and the cavity sealed with waterproof adhesive. The pot is raised on feet to allow the wire to pass beneath.*

2 *The pump is placed in position in the center of the pot. Modern submersible pumps are ideal for restricted conditions and are easily adjusted to provide an accurate water flow. At this point, test the flow of the pump while it is still accessible.*

3 *Measure the depth of the pot so that an accurate assessment can be made of the dimensions required for the wire support.*

4 *Various supports can be used, but the most useful is a standard wire plant support for the herbaceous border with its legs reduced in length. These can be easily removed with wire cutters.*

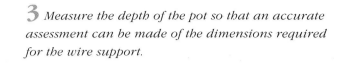

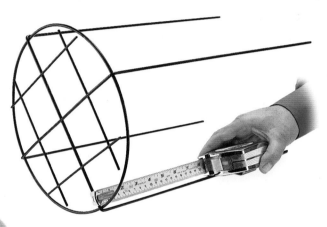

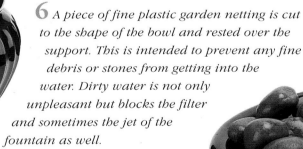

5 *The support is placed in the pot with the outfall of the pump emerging from the center. There should be sufficient room to the rim of the pot to allow for the stones.*

6 *A piece of fine plastic garden netting is cut to the shape of the bowl and rested over the support. This is intended to prevent any fine debris or stones from getting into the water. Dirty water is not only unpleasant but blocks the filter and sometimes the jet of the fountain as well.*

A simple but very classy contained water feature.

7 *Clean stones are placed evenly around the fountain jet. This disguises the netting and permits water to flow back for recirculating. The stones can be built up in the center so that the water emerges from their midst.*

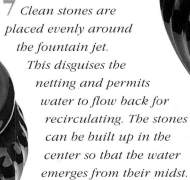

terracotta and glazed pots

Terracotta and ceramic pots can make a most imaginative addition to the garden when used with water. Generally utilized for shrubs and border plants, with some adaptation they can be used to create a wide diversity of water features – not only planted arrangements, but imaginative displays with moving water.

Manufacturers have realized how wonderfully these pots and water complement one another and now regularly

Right: The glazed pot planted with a single dwarf waterlily forms a centerpiece and focal point for this sunken decked area. The circular walls, paths and semi-circular backdrop echo the aquatic centerpiece. It is important with a feature such as this to maintain water clarity by regularly siphoning off and replacing some of the water. It is never practical to attempt to create a natural balance in such a small volume of water.

Left: With a little inventiveness an interesting water feature can be created with a series of traditional clay plant pots inverted upon one another with a pump placed in a sump below, and the outlet pipe taken up the center.

make provisions for the inclusion of a pump or tubing in their designs as well as producing pots without drainage holes. In some cases the pots and accessories that are necessary to create a moving water feature are offered for sale as a kit with instructions. These are a little limiting in their range, and so the more individualistic gardener will want to select an original pot and make adaptations personally.

While these beautiful pots are excellent for moving
water, they are also most accommodating of planting.
The best effects are created by individual plant types
being grown in single pots, and then grouped together
in a pleasing fashion. Being mobile, they are very versatile.
An early spring-flowering pot of marsh marigolds, for
example, can be replaced with a summer one of iris when
the marsh marigolds' foliage starts to look jaded.

miniature pot pool

One of the most attractive contained water features is the miniature pool in a pot or bowl. This can be successfully established outside in the garden, although it is often thought more suited to the conservatory. For management purposes it is best stood outdoors, since the water remains cooler and the plants grow more in character.

The establishment of such a feature is quite simple and there are some very interesting pygmy plants which can be grown in a confined space. It is good management that is vital if it is to be a success. There is nothing complicated about this; just remember that it is important to attend to the feature very regularly, almost daily if it is to remain in pristine condition. A few days of neglect and water quality will deteriorate. When this happens with such a small volume of water, it can have disastrous implications for both plants and fish.

Not that fish are essential, for the pot pool can exist perfectly well without, and with such a small amount of water there is little opportunity of striking a natural balance. However, a solitary goldfish can perform a most valuable task in such a water feature, since it is the most efficient and biologically friendly way of controlling the inevitable mosquito larvae that will find their way into the water.

PLANTING A POT POOL

1 *The base of the pot can be covered with stones to the required depth. These will bring the small container-grown plants to the right level, 2-3 in. (5-8 cm) below the rim of the pot. The stones will also be effective in trapping debris which can be periodically and easily siphoned out. The water in a pot pool will require regular replacement.*

2 *Position the plants carefully, making sure that they all stand securely. Choose a variety of plants that are happy in the same depth of water.*

3 *Add water without disturbing the plants. Topping up with water because of evaporation will be a regular occurrence and periodic siphoning may be necessary if the water turns green.*

4 *The completed planting makes an attractive feature for terrace, patio or balcony. A similar arrangement can be contrived for indoors if the plants are suitable.*

····· PLANTING SUGGESTIONS ·····

Plants Used

Ceratophyllum demersum/submerged
Eriophorum angustifolium/summer/marginal
Iris laevigata/summer/marginal
Zantedeschia aethiopica 'Kiwi Blush'/
summer/marginal

Alternative Plants

Myriophyllum proserpinacoides/summer/
marginal
Nymphaea 'Pygmaea Helvola'/
summer/waterlily
Pontederia cordata/late summer/marginal
Typha minima/summer/marginal

Left: *A potful of aquatic beauty. A single pygmy waterlily is growing freely in a decorative glazed pot.*

pot fountains

Traditionally most of us regard fountains as jets of water which shoot into the air, almost a form of aquatic sculpture if you consider the different forms that the jets can create. Sometimes they emerge from an otherwise still water surface, although we are also quite used to seeing elaborate figures – be they human, animal or mythical – spouting water from the most unlikely places.

It therefore comes as a refreshing change, when considering moving water for our smaller gardens, to discover that there are a whole range of free-standing fountains incorporated into Ali Baba pots, urns and other containers that will fulfill our desire for moving water, but which can be placed on the smallest terrace or patio. They only need to be filled with water and plugged into an outlet to be fully operational.

Below: Traditional pots can make pleasing small formal arrangements. The water flows evenly over the pots and into the surrounding gravel, beneath which the sump and pump are located. The surrounding plants are growing in moist soil, but need not necessarily be bog garden subjects.

Above: *Although the chutes of water are important and create wonderful sound, they are mere acolytes to the central urn with its impressive bubbler. Separate pumps operate the urn and wall water feature, while the tasteful planting softens the scene.*

Left: *Pot fountains only work well when water clarity and pot cleanliness are high priorities. For an even flow and distribution, it is essential that the rim of the pot is level.*

Pot fountains in their many colors and configurations are ideal for intimate parts of the garden which can be reached by an electricity supply. Placed beside a seat beneath a leafy bower, an urn gently spilling water over its rim into a cobbled base graced with ferns creates an ambiance as close to heaven as we are likely to enjoy here on Earth.

ali baba fountain

If you really want to be classy, then you can go for a mystical eastern look or a warm Mediterranean effect with an Ali Baba fountain. Tall jars and pots imported from abroad make wonderful features in a western garden. But they needn't be confined to a western style, since on a modern patio or deck they can often be incorporated into the garden scene unconventionally, the overall picture being built around the featured pots.

When selecting a suitable pot for such a feature, its outer appearance is vital. It must have strong color and presence, yet be able to accommodate the necessary tubing to permit the establishment of sufficient water flow to create the desired effect. There can be a considerable lift for a pump, depending upon where it is placed, and it is essential that the capacity together with the lift and flow required is carefully considered before the pump is purchased. An excess of capacity is desirable.

Ali Baba fountains are not year-round features in colder climates, for few of the large pots that are available to the home gardener are sufficiently frostproof to tolerate freezing when full of water without shaling, flaking or fracturing. As winter approaches, drain off the water and seal the top to prevent snow and rain entering if you wish to leave the pot outside. Otherwise take it indoors for protection.

Right: While most Ali Baba fountains use the container to make a statement, this sunken version depends on two strong jets of water dressed beneath with glass and pebbles.

MAKING AN ALI BABA FOUNTAIN

2 The submersible pump is placed in the sump prior to the top being replaced and the jar positioned. The electrical cord is disguised as much as possible.

1 As the central flow of water must be accurately controlled, the pump outlet must be secured to a fixed copper pipe.

3 Bricks put into the base of the pot help to hold the copper pipe in position. The pipe must be central in the jar so that the bubble of water appears in the middle.

4 *Feed the hose from the pump through the base of the jar and connect it to the copper pipe. Seal the hole in the jar with a waterproof sealer.*

5 *Finally position the jar ensuring that the rim is level to ensure an even overflow. Dress around the base and disguise the sump with fine cobbles.*

A solitary jar softly weeping and sparkling in the summer sun. The lilies add fragrance.

bamboo spout fountain

The Oriental look is very fashionable now and bamboo looks particularly effective when used to make a fountain in association with simple glazed pottery. There are a wide range of bamboo canes available which can serve as pipes to carry water if the dividing sections between the solid leaf nodes or joints are cut or drilled through to permit the water to flow along the length of the bamboo cane. In many cases the distances between the leaf joints are sufficiently long that you can establish a suitable up-stand or spout without the need for drilling.

A most attractive simple indoor feature can be created by taking a length of bamboo and splicing in a spout of bamboo of smaller dimensions. The spout should be of sufficient diameter to accommodate a narrow flexible tube that will be attached to a submersible pump. The tube leads from the pump, up through the larger diameter section of bamboo and fits neatly into the spout. It is ideal if the tube and spout are of roughly the same diameter, but, if not, the tube can be glued into the spout with sealant without it showing.

The upright pipe should be sited next to the small submersible pump and wedged into the pot in a vertical position with large stones. The pump sits neatly on the floor of the pot with large stones placed around it so that it is effectively in a small chamber. Further stones are added and a decorative layer of pebbles included as top dressing. Water is then poured into the pot to a depth that ensures that the pump is completely submerged. The pump circulates the water up through the bamboo and out of the spout back into the pot in a circular flow. Evaporation will lower the water level over time, so check regularly to see if the water needs topping up.

MAKING A BAMBOO SPOUT FOUNTAIN

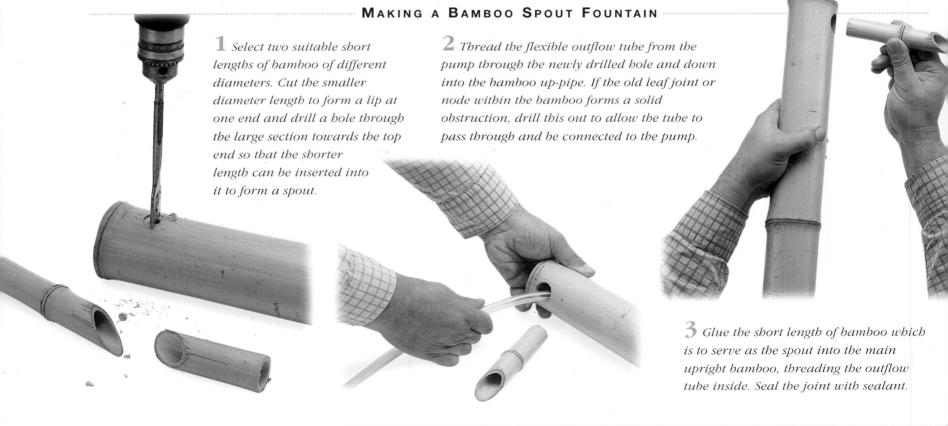

1 Select two suitable short lengths of bamboo of different diameters. Cut the smaller diameter length to form a lip at one end and drill a hole through the large section towards the top end so that the shorter length can be inserted into it to form a spout.

2 Thread the flexible outflow tube from the pump through the newly drilled hole and down into the bamboo up-pipe. If the old leaf joint or node within the bamboo forms a solid obstruction, drill this out to allow the tube to pass through and be connected to the pump.

3 Glue the short length of bamboo which is to serve as the spout into the main upright bamboo, threading the outflow tube inside. Seal the joint with sealant.

4 Position the bamboo upright in the pot using two or three large stones to wedge it in place. Ensure the outflow tube is not pinched.

5 Place the pump on the bottom of the pot and connect it to the outflow tube that runs up inside the bamboo.

6 Position a wire support next to the bamboo upright. This wedges into the pot about two-thirds of the way up.

7 Place a selection of large polished stones onto the wire support in order to disguise it and so that a water chamber is created for the pump below. The pot is then filled with water to just beneath the level of the stones.

Below: *Here the water flows over the pot and through the cobbles into a reservoir below.*

Left: *The finished fountain will need regular topping up.*

bamboo spout

Traditional Far Eastern bamboo spouts and deer scarers – hinged bamboo spouts that strike a stone when empty, thereby creating a noise to scare away wild animals from crops – were often connected to large established water features. But those that are used to adorn contemporary gardens are generally container water features; with modern technology they are able to stand alone independently of a water garden. Indeed they are often most effective when established by themselves in dappled shade surrounded by lush ferns.

At the garden center, it is common to come across moving bamboo water spouts sold as a package, complete with sump and reinforced netting cover, the submersible pump and cobbles included. Indeed, it is the submersible pump which has revolutionized this kind of feature, since it is merely placed in the sump beneath the water which is circulated through the bamboo. Evaporation causes some loss of water, but for the most part the system is very efficient and effective.

If you wish something more innovative than the traditional deer scarer or *shishi odoshi,* then it is simple to create your own feature with water tumbling from one cane to the other, providing that the last drop to the cobbles on the ground is immediately over the sump which contains the submersible pump. Otherwise the opportunities for creating a contained bamboo water feature are only limited by the imagination.

Right: *It is possible to obtain a wide range of authentic Japanese artifacts to enhance an Oriental water feature. This paving tile represents the season of autumn.*

1 *The pump is positioned in the sump over which the stone bowl is to be placed. The internal load-bearing supports must be sufficiently robust.*

2 *Place the stone bowl in position so that water will flow from the area of the lip as desired. Tilt it slightly forward to assist this.*

3 *Place cobbles around the bowl to disguise the sump and to provide secure support for the bowl.*

4 *Position the supports. These are two bamboo canes of equal length bound together with twine or raffia to form a rest.*

5 *Having positioned both supports, take the delivery cane and place it in position on the rests. The hose delivering the water runs up the cane at the back of the spout.*

Right: Another option for a bamboo spout where space is very limited. This is based upon similar construction principles.

····· PLANTING SUGGESTIONS ·····

Plants Used

Dryopteris affinis/fern

Pleioblastus okinosasa/dwarf bamboo

Alternative Plants

Fargesia nitida/bamboo

Matteuccia struthiopteris/fern

Arundinaria pumila/dwarf bamboo

Pleioblastus viride-striata/bamboo

6 *Secure the end of the bamboo water spout and insert the delivery hose of the pump. Test once again. Dress with rocks and plants.*

7 *The completed water spout. It is a charming and simple Orientally themed water feature which can become an integral part of a garden landscape or rest easily alone. It is inexpensive and easy to construct and requires minimal maintenance.*

sunken containers

There is a misconception that if you create a water feature in a container, it has to be situated above ground. That is not so, for small volumes of water can equally well be accommodated sunk into the ground. Indeed, there are positive practical advantages, for when below ground level there is little danger of the container being damaged by frost, and the wildlife inhabitants harmed by prolonged freezing. Perhaps surprisingly the winter temperature of a small volume of water in the ground is several degrees higher than that in a container above soil level.

Sinking a container hides it from view. The only practical concern is that the depth and volume of water are sufficient to permit you to create or grow whatever you fancy. Visually it is the surface area shape that is of concern. It matters little what the sunken container is made of, or whether it served a completely different purpose in a previous life. Thus old baths and cisterns are commonly pressed into use along with plastic storage boxes and garbage containers.

The innovative gardener does not necessarily require a waterproof vessel, since wire trays can be used in an excavation and then lined with ordinary pool liner. The effect is the same as that of a sunken container.

Right: *This is a beautifully arranged water feature which demonstrates excellent proportions and conformity with its surroundings. Although the focal water body appears to be quite sophisticated, it is in reality a simple container sunk into the ground and dressed around with very large, flat stones. The strategically placed boulders and clever associated planting through the gravel create an air of quality and sophistication. Dressing the container with plants is unnecessary as the fountain draws the eye to the center and provides activity.*

Left: *Although this is clearly a container, it is sunk almost up to its rim and the peripheral planting extended to the edge to unite it with the surrounding garden. The advantage of sinking a container is that during the summer the body of water is cool and in winter it is not so vulnerable to frost.*

making a sunken container

Mention container water gardens and people tend to assume that the container will be sited above the ground. There is no reason why it should not be sunk into it. Sinking a container presents the opportunity of utilizing unsightly but functional containers which you would not normally consider. It also provides much easier opportunities for creating discrete and hidden reservoirs of water from which a pump can operate. Sinking the container also protects the inhabitants from harsh winter weather and in some circumstances permits fish to overwinter outdoors successfully.

When sinking a container it is important to ensure that it is well supported by the surrounding soil. Not all containers are of a conventional square or rounded shape; some are of a very irregular configuration. Apart from ensuring stability, it is also as important with a contained water garden to guarantee that it is level from side to side and end to end so that there is no undesirable overflow.

Sunken containers are rather like conventional pools, so all the precautions that are taken when creating a garden pool should be observed if success is to be assured. However, although many of the rules of the pool follow here, because the volume of water used is so small, there is no prospect of plants being arranged so that the water body can maintain a natural ecological balance. Evaporation and rapid temperature changes prevent this.

A SUNKEN CONTAINER POOL

1 *A simple storage container can be utilized to create a most effective pool when sunk into the ground.*

2 *Make sure that the container is level from side to side and end to end. Back-fill firmly and create a level area around.*

3 *Make a sand and cement mortar mix and trowel it around the top of the container to provide a bed for tiling edges.*

4 *Lay the tiles evenly around the container making sure that there is a slight overhang which will disguise the edge. Ensure that they are completely level.*

5 *Place the plants into the pool before filling it with water. Use only dwarf varieties.*

PLANTING SUGGESTIONS

Plants Used

Eriophorum angustifolium/summer/marginal

Juncus ensifolius/summer/marginal

Mentha cervina alba/summer/marginal

Nymphaea 'Pygmaea Helvola'/summer/waterlily

Alternative Plants

Carex pendula/summer/marginal

Houttuynia cordata/summer/marginal

Myosotis scorpioides/summer/marginal

Typha minima/summer/marginal

6 *The completed pool will require regular maintenance as the volume of water is too small to sustain a natural balance.*

This sunken pool uses aquatic plants to create a balanced and harmonious feature. If you prefer a more lively effect, it is easy to position a small submersible pump to create a fountain or small water cascade.

Right: *Whatever your fancy, a small pool can be created with a container of any kind providing that it is liberally dressed with plants. There is no indication of the construction materials used in this simple but attractive feature.*

formal features

Formal water gardening tends to be very much more about the water than plants or fish, although both can make valuable contributions to a formal feature. Open water with a glassy stillness that reflects all about it, and the sparkling spray from a strategically placed fountain, are hallmarks of a modern formal water garden.

Symmetrically designed, a formal water garden usually consists of a square, rectangle, circle or oval, or an evenly arranged combination of two or more of these elements. The positions of a fountain, ornaments and plants are arranged so that the overall appearance is one of balance. Edging is also uniform and formal in style, often assisting in creating a clear-cut look with neatly defined boundaries which adds to its formality.

Formal water features only rest easily in formal gardens where the pool shape and the various beds and borders complement one another. While frequently created in a lawn, the formal pool is at its most versatile set among hard landscaping, being valuable in assisting with changes in level in the garden, especially where moving water can be employed to take advantage of any gradient. While plants are sometimes used to enhance the formal effect, very often the pool is devoid of aquatic plant life and exists merely to mirror its surroundings.

Apart from strictly formal arrangements, there are also semi-formal water gardens that are used to make a satisfactory transition from the formal garden neighboring a house to the informal surrounding landscape. These are more difficult to create because they straddle two different design styles, but when done well are among the most rewarding of all water features to contemplate.

Perfect symmetry and a clever use of perspective combine to create a beautifully balanced formal effect.

classical-style square pools

The classical formal pool originated in Greece and Italy. Rather as with traditional Moorish and Arabic styles, it grew out of a need to irrigate crops in a reliable way. Usually the spring from where the water originated became an early kind of water garden, a temple honoring a god or goddess perhaps being constructed nearby. Trees were planted and in due course a garden added. As more elaboration with channels and basins arose, statuary was added, not just for ornament, but in order to propel water in jets or streams.

The Romans incorporated the best elements of the Greek pleasure garden into their villa gardens, and the use of water for purely decorative purposes was born. Aqueducts and fountains were used freely and many can still be seen functioning in the great cities of Italy. The channels and rills of the Greeks and Italians developed into canal-like ponds, while influences from India and the Far East led to the establishment of square and rectangular ponds, often with seating areas within them where in hot weather a cooler atmosphere could be enjoyed. Often these island-like seating places were linked by stepping stones, the pond being used for recreation rather than primarily for visual appeal as in the present day garden.

Right: *Ponds like this originally arose from the need to irrigate a garden, but eventually they became ornamental centerpieces in their own right. The upright conifers lend a Mediterranean feel to the garden scene and reflect the period when formally arranged trees were often associated with water.*

Below left: *An unplanted canal-like pool with a formally planted waterside. The open water is intended to reflect all about it, at the same time helping to provide an illusion of distance within the garden. Often pools of this type narrow at the far end in order to give an illusion of distance to a small plot.*

Left: *An attractive formal arrangement. The paved area and pool are in proportion to one another and the symmetrically arranged clumps of aquatic irises stand guard alongside the fountain mask.*

Modern square or rectangular pools are generally constructed to fit into the garden landscape. The pool shape reflects the contours of those parts of the garden which lie adjacent, whether they be bed, border or lawn. Often they are constructed to serve as mirrors, the water reflecting the garden in its glassy stillness. They are rarely planted, except for one or two clumps of strategically placed waterlilies and perhaps corners bristling with spiky reeds.

classical-style round pools

There is no reliable precedent for the round or curved pool although it probably evolved from the Greek nymphaeum – a grotto or shrine sacred to the nymphs. Throughout history circular and curved pools have appeared in garden design, the circular ones tending to be purely for reflection of the sky while the curved kinds have often delineated other parts of the garden or been home to an array of fountains or fountain statuary.

Fountains are often incorporated into circular pools too, and one of the most impressive sights in the formal garden is a circular pool with a single jet of water arising from its center. A pool devoid of plants and highlighted by a silvery plume of water twisting in the bright sunlight has a magic all of its own.

Circular pools, unlike square and rectangular configurations, usually stand alone. Classical styles generally have a raised surround, often with elaborate ornamentation and this can be achieved by using one of the very fine reconstituted stone products which are obtainable from garden centers nowadays. Available in sectional form, they are easily assembled and have much of the grandeur associated with the historic past.

Similarly fountain ornaments of classical design for circular ponds are often faithful, although scaled-down, reproductions of famous fountains and lend a touch of majesty to the most modest plot.

Right: This circular pool retains its air of formality despite the cluttered arrangement of floating and marginal plants.

Below: *Raised ponds of a symmetrical construction usually rest quite easily in the garden landscape.*

Right: *This simple circular raised pond is the focal point of the entire garden. So much depends upon its proportions and planting arrangement for the overall picture to be a success. The containers reflect the shape of the pond and themselves make circular contributions to a garden dominated by circles. The two small trees stand as sentinels guarding the approach to the pond from the outer garden.*

marking out the site

Having selected a suitable site, the first task is to mark out the position of the pool accurately. For a liner pool this can be done with a series of strings, pegs and simple mathematical formulas which most of us learned at school. When employing a liner it is important to be very accurate with the size and profile of the pool, especially if the liner is prepurchased. Experienced water gardeners often create the excavation and then measure accurately to ensure that any unexpected vagaries in the excavation are accounted for when the length of liner to be bought is calculated.

Apart from ensuring accuracy of form, it is important to get the pool level. Even a small deviation can cause both water spillage on one side and exposure of the inner pool-side on the other. Position a mean level peg and then work from this with a board and level, ensuring that the whole area is accurately assessed. Soil can then be redistributed according to the various levels indicated by the pegs. When installing a liner it is preferable to take the lowest point in the leveling process and to transfer the mean level peg to that position. Although it is possible to raise levels by filling with soil, when using a liner it is preferable to excavate so that the soil profile remains undisturbed, thereby enabling a solid excavation to be achieved.

With a preformed pool this is not so critical, although accurate leveling is just as vital. While there are recommendations which suggest that an excavation can be accurately created to accommodate the shelves of a preformed pool, it is generally preferable to dig a hole that embraces the maximum length, breadth and depths of the pool and to position it within the all-embracing hole. Backfiling to fill in any voids in the soil once the preformed pool is in place is usually easiest with pea-gravel. This leaves a considerable quantity of soil to dispose of around the garden. If there is too much to redistribute, then it is best to take it away rather than create a clay mound with a few added stones and optimistically call it a rock garden.

MARKING OUT AN OVAL

1 *Knock in pegs at both ends, and one in the center. Add two more at two-thirds the distance between the center and end pegs.*

2 *Tie a length of string around four of the pegs – not all five. This establishes the correct length for the marker.*

3 *Now loop this length of string around the three inner pegs and take up the slack with a sharp piece of bamboo cane.*

4 *Making sure that the string is held taut, score a line in the turf with the bamboo moving in a curve around the center peg.*

5 *As you move around towards the end peg, the cane will naturally inscribe an oval shape on the ground.*

6 *To make the outline clear, sprinkle sand freely along it.*

MARKING A CIRCLE

1 *Place a peg in the center of the intended circle. Attach a string and use a second cane to inscribe the circumference.*

2 *Use sand to distinguish the score mark clearly in the turf. It also gives a good impression of how the finished pool will fit into the garden plan.*

Left: *This formal arrangement shows clearly the skills of the mathematician and surveyor and is something to which the formal water gardener may wish to aspire. If the component parts are tackled separately, using simple marking-out techniques, in reality such intricate layouts are not as difficult to create as they may at first appear.*

A right angle can be created by marking out a triangle using Pythagoras' 3-4-5 system of measurement.

ESTABLISHING LEVELS

1 *You must establish the levels of the ground where the pool is to be dug. Set a datum peg to the desired level, and use more pegs and a spirit level to establish the horizontal.*

2 *Measure the distance to the ground of your first datum peg. This is the level at which you want all the edges of the pool to sit when it has been excavated.*

3 *Now transfer this measurement to the other pegs in all directions across the site. This shows where the soil needs cutting away or filling up to establish a flat surround.*

making a round lined pool

A circular pool is slightly more difficult to construct using a liner than one which is square or oblong, largely because it is more complicated to make the necessary folds of the liner so that they are unobtrusive. However, in every other respect it follows the methods used for the less complex liner constructions of square formal ponds.

Marking out is achieved simply by using the two stakes and string method – a central stake has a string attached which is the radius of the pool, and attached to the end of this is a sharpened stake which scores out the position of the pool edge as it is scribed around the central peg in a circle. A trickle of sand can be used to delineate the outline more clearly if necessary. The depth and shelving arrangements should then be calculated and a quantity of liner purchased based upon the maximum length and breadth of the finished pool (measurements which are of course identical for a circular pool) plus twice the maximum depth.

The site of the excavation must be made level or else there will be water spillage from the pool at one point and liner exposure at the opposite side. It is much simpler to prepare for this before digging begins than to try to rectify it when the liner has been laid and water added. The excavation should also ideally be created in undisturbed soil so that it can be carved out without minor soil movements. Thus it is always preferable when leveling the site to reduce a higher area rather than to add soil to a low-lying part.

The excavation is made to precisely the dimensions of the intended final pool, any sharp stones or other debris being carefully removed and protective pool underlay fabric installed. Damp bricklayers' sand can also be used to form a protective cushion, but this is not so useful where there are significant steep sides to cater for.

EXCAVATING A ROUND POOL

1 *Mark out a circle on the ground using two pegs and a piece of string which is the length of the radius of the finished pool.*

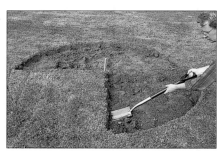

2 *Remove the turf to produce the outline of the pool. Use a sharp spade or a turfing iron to make a neat job of the excavation.*

3 *It is important that the excavation is level as this will provide the pool profile. Check with a board and level regularly.*

4 *Ensure that the marginal shelves are level across the excavation in each direction and of the correct depth.*

5 *Scour the excavation and remove any sharp stones, twigs or other objects which may pierce the liner under the weight of water.*

6 *As an added precaution to guard against puncture, a layer of sand can be spread over the base of the excavation and the shelves.*

Above: *A beautiful pool can be created easily and economically with a liner. Once established, it has a look of permanence usually associated with a concrete construction.*

7 *The completed excavation is carefully lined with pond liner underlay. Water it to help it conform to the shape of the hole.*

8 *The pool liner is placed as accurately as possible within the hole. Large regular folds are then made to eliminate creases.*

9 *Water is added. As the water rises, the folds can be adjusted and any small creases or wrinkles in the liner smoothed out.*

making a round lined pool

The liner should be spread out to warm in the summer sun before being introduced to the excavated hole. This makes it much more malleable and eases the problem of making neat folds when the time comes to do this. Water is then added and the liner begins to stretch to accommodate itself to the excavation. At this stage creases should be smoothed away as far as possible and the folds in the liner made to help it conform to the shape of the hole. Once the water level has reached the top, the liner edge can be trimmed so that it can be disguised beneath paving or whatever edging is intended.

The method by which a preformed pool is installed is not dissimilar, except that the excavation should be larger and embrace the entire pool with space to spare for backfilling. Pools made from vacuum-formed plastic have little rigidity, so water must be added as backfilling takes place; otherwise the soft plastic walls of the pool will buckle inwards. While it has been traditional to backfill with soil from the excavation site, much better results are achieved with the use of pea gravel, which flows easily between the sides of the pool and the soil. This avoids creating any voids or air pockets, a common problem if lumpy, uncompromising clay soil from the excavation is used.

As with a lined pool, a preformed pool should be installed with the edges level to avoid water spillage. The level should be checked regularly during the backfilling process as a preformed pool will move as the pea gravel flows around. Always allow play of about 1 inch (2.5 cm) for the pool to rise within the excavation as backfilling takes place.

Above: *This circular pool is neatly edged with paving. The use of specially manufactured paving slabs which are deliberately curved makes a neat circular construction such as this relatively straightforward to build.*

EDGING THE POOL

1 *Paving slabs provide the best formal edging. Allow a small overhang to produce a neat edge and remove any surplus liner.*

2 *Excavate the area beneath the slab and liner and fill back to ground level with mortar. Poolside paving must be very secure.*

3 *Lay the slabs and ensure that they are level in every direction. Point the gaps between them evenly with mortar.*

Right: *Paving is a neat method of finishing the edge of a circular pool, but it can also be an integral part of the garden scene. Here the extensive paved areas add much to the beauty of the pool, extending its influence into the surrounding garden landscape. They also provide safe and ready access for the enjoyment of the pool, the adjacent areas also being of sufficient size to permit recreation and relaxation at the waterside. The planting in and around the margins of the pool helps to soften its contours.*

installing an external filter

External filters permit the regular treatment of pond water and produce excellent results. Most extract solid debris, and also pass the water through bio-blocks or similar material where helpful aerobic bacteria convert toxic ammonia into nitrites and ultimately nitrates. If a carbon-impregnated pad is included in the outflow, then organic wastes can be completely eliminated from the water.

External filters can be positioned on the surface of the ground next to the pool and discreetly hidden by vegetation. However, it is neater to sink them into the ground, accommodation often being made for them in a purpose-built chamber near the summit of a waterfall. It is wise to create a firm base by using a paving slab or bricks so that the filter box is level in its chamber.

Once the filter box has been positioned, the lid can be replaced and the hole backfilled taking care not to disturb the box. When a UV filter is included to kill algae in the water, this can be accommodated next to the main filter box. It is then necessary to run the filter feed hose into the pool; if the filter is situated close to the top of a waterfall it is most appropriate to conceal the hose at the base of the waterfall.

The bio-filter and UV filter can then be connected and the pump attached to the filter feed hose. Once the pump is turned on, the filtration process begins. It will take four to six weeks in warm weather before the biological part of the filter establishes sufficient beneficial bacteria for the process of breaking down the harmful toxins in the water to get underway and the pond chemistry starts to improve.

INSTALLING AN EXTERNAL FILTER

1 *First excavate the area where you want to sink the filter chamber into the ground.*

2 *Use a paving slab or a layer of bricks to provide a firm and level base for the filter.*

3 *Put the filter chamber in position. Ensure that it is level and secure before backfilling.*

4 *Replace the lid and backfill around the sides using either soil or fine pea gravel.*

5 *If the filter has a UV option, attach this close to the main filter chamber. It is then easily accessible when required.*

6 *With the UV attachment in place, run the filter feed hose into the pool. When the filter is positioned close to a waterfall as is illustrated here, it is easiest to conceal the hose in the rocks at the base of the waterfall.*

7 *The pump is then attached to the filter. Make sure that the pump is powerful enough to operate the filter effectively.*

8 *Run the pump to make sure that it works properly. The biological filter will take several weeks to become fully effective.*

Above: *Excavations are not always necessary in order to successfully accommodate a filter. Rather than concealing it in the ground, the filter in this delightful formal arrangement is disguised by lush vegetation.*

9 *It is a good idea to position some plants around the filter that will grow up and hide it from view. Once the filter is working efficiently, water clarity in the pool can almost be assured.*

raised pools

There are a number of reasons, apart from purely aesthetic ones, why it is desirable to have a raised pool. On a conventional level site, height can be a useful design asset. It also provides the fish with greater protection from predator animals and herons. There is some merit also in the fact that it is difficult for children to tumble into the water accidentally, although if a low wall is part of the pool, this may prove a tempting attraction for children who will want to run along it.

A raised pool which is built so that it is contained by a conventional wall is a fascinating feature, since it brings the pool nearer to the observer. There are few greater pleasures in a garden than to sit on the edge of a raised pool on a warm summer day dabbling one's fingers in the cool water and observing the fish as they glide effortlessly beneath verdant waterlily pads.

Below: *This is quite a simple pool to construct. Here concrete blockwork has been attractively rendered with a cement mix.*

Above: *This pool is an important decorative feature in its garden. Plants are important, but visually the pool would benefit if they were reduced so that the clear water surface could be enjoyed more.*

While raised pools can be desirable in themselves, they can also serve to link parts of the garden that are at differing levels. Rather than the conventional stream or waterfall, raised pools of varying heights can link levels in a terracing effect, water tumbling from one to another. Even still water contained at different levels provides a visual link. Raised pool features can even be recessed into a slope and slightly raised above it; where appropriate, steps can be incorporated in the same way as one might in a conventional terraced garden feature.

A sloping site also provides an opportunity for using innovative formal designs where triangles, rhomboids and parallelograms can with imagination be incorporated comfortably into an overall garden scheme. For the most part, it is only in the formal garden with a sloping aspect that such configurations rest easy.

making a raised pool

There are many options for building a raised pool, ranging from a standard brick or stone wall construction to a timber sleeper arrangement. It is possible to use an existing watertight vessel, such as a header tank, and build around it, or the feature may be created from scratch. For the inventive gardener the latter option is to be preferred, since the pool can then be exactly what is required rather than the inevitable compromise offered by a container disguised by a surrounding wall.

As with pools that are sunk in the ground, it is important to have a level base from which to work with a raised pool. Remember that the underlying level of the ground is transferred upwards with a raised pool and the problems of spillage and liner exposure are potentially the same.

Of all the construction materials that are available, properly preserved timber is the most versatile and also the most resistant to severe winter weather. In areas where hard or prolonged frosts are common, a brick construction can suffer badly from fracturing owing to the expansion of the ice in freezing conditions, or shaling of the surface of the bricks (unless engineering bricks are used). Timber is a warmer material visually and also has sufficient flexibility in it to withstand movement within the pool caused by the freezing of ice.

Installing a liner is very easy in a timber pool, since it can be readily secured to the internal wooden walls using a narrow batten to trap the liner, which is then secured with roofing nails.

MAKING A RAISED TIMBER POOL

1 *Place the sleeper timbers in a square arrangement. Ensure that each one overlaps the junction between the timbers below it.*

2 *Secure the timbers in place with strong metal strips or ties. Use self-tapping screws and an electric screwdriver.*

3 *Measure the pool liner and fit it accurately into the structure, making bold folds in the corners to minimize creasing.*

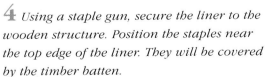

4 *Using a staple gun, secure the liner to the wooden structure. Position the staples near the top edge of the liner. They will be covered by the timber batten.*

5 *Align the timber batten with the top edge of the timber structure so as to trap the liner in place. Secure it with roofing nails.*

6 *Create a marginal planting pocket by putting a square of liner underlay in a corner and build a box-like structure with loose bricks.*

7 *Once the container area has been completed, add good garden soil or aquatic planting compost. Plant into this and top dress with pea gravel.*

8 *The completed pool. Architectural plants like bulrush and pickerel have been used to add a strong vertical note to the feature.*

Goldfish and shubunkins bring the pool to life and control insect pests.

Right: *A raised pool makes a strong statement in this garden.*

····· PLANTING SUGGESTIONS ·····

Plants Used

Acorus calamus 'Variegatus'/summer/marginal
Caltha palustris polypetala/spring/marginal
Nymphaea 'Laydekeri Lilacea'/summer
Pontederia cordata/summer/marginal
Schoenoplectus tabernaemontani/summer/
marginal

Alternative Plants

Canna glauca hybrids/summer/marginal
Houttuynia cordata/summer/marginal
Iris laevigata 'Variegata'/summer/marginal
Juncus effusus 'Spiralis'/summer/marginal
Mentha cervina/summer/marginal
Nymphaea 'Gloriosa'/summer/aquatic

installing a formal patio pool

There are many opportunities for creating a small water feature on a patio. It is mostly undesirable to excavate a pool in such a position, as the soil is unlikely to be compacted and stable, a prerequisite when using a liner. It is more likely that a layer of hardcore will need to be removed before soil level is reached. Apart from such vagaries of construction, which need not dissuade the enthusiast from creating such a pool if it is deemed an essential part of the garden's design, a sunken pool in a patio will gather all sorts of leaves and debris that blow into it. A raised pool not only alleviates all these practical problems, but offers the gardener the opportunity to enjoy the beauty of the plants and activities of the fish closer to hand.

Raised pools available to the home gardener are generally of simple construction, but they are very effective. They are usually round, octagonal or occasionally square and consist either of a rigid container around which an outer decorative surround is built, or are of a modular construction, usually of timber, which is lined with a pool liner that is secured internally with wooden battens or carpet strip. While the majority depend upon a conventional lining, there are now constructions in which the pool liner is preformed and welded into a shape which drops into the structure, where it fits exactly without any need for folds or tucks.

As with a pool which is excavated in the ground, the raised pool demands a level surface. In kit form, the modern raised patio pool is of very straightforward construction and is one of the most satisfactory formal water features when constraints of space demand a small-scale construction for the terrace or patio.

MAKING A SELF-BUILD PATIO POOL

1 *The preformed timber sections are already treated with a preservative, but are bland and uninteresting. Garden stains or wood paints help brighten its appearance.*

2 *Small metal fasteners are screwed into the main bearers, both at the top and the bottom. These provide the structure with rigidity. It is important that they are accurately installed.*

Above: *Apart from self-assembly patio pools, many other small-scale DIY water features are available. This bubbling pot fountain sits on top of a water reservoir hidden beneath the cobbles.*

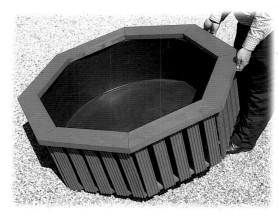

3 *When most of the sections have been screwed together, the tub which forms the pool is slid into the prepared framework. The final fixings are then made.*

4 *Once the whole pool structure is complete, it can be positioned. It is important to have a level situation, such as a terrace, on which to site it permanently.*

5 *Fill the pool with water. It looks best if the final level in such a pool is established an inch or so beneath the overhang of the top surround.*

6 *If a pump is to be installed, create a small level plinth with a few loose housebricks. The depth is determined by the length of the fountain attachment.*

7 *Position the pump centrally and ensure that the top of the fountain nozzle is just above the water surface. Take care to hide the electrical cord as neatly as possible.*

8 *Switch the pump on and adjust the spray height to suit the space available. Water splash and the height of the jet in relation to its surroundings should be considered.*

Oriental-style water gardens

The Oriental style of gardening uses water freely. Although nowadays most gardeners associate it with Japanese gardening, it was the Chinese who first developed the theme many centuries ago, from where it migrated to Japan as Buddhism spread. Chinese art forms, including garden design, reached Japan in the 6th and 7th centuries AD. The Chinese influence gradually declined and by the 17th century a distinctive Japanese style, which borrowed the original theme of man's relationship with nature had evolved. This was more precise and symbolic, and emanated very much from Zen Buddhist monks.

Below: Everything in this Oriental garden is positioned precisely and with meaning. The rocks represent mountains, the trees forests and the pool a lake. The seat is positioned in an ideal place for quiet

Oriental gardens use water to add beauty and tranquillity, to create a place where people can contemplate and observe nature and discover their place in the natural order. A calm, reflecting surface of water is intended to expand one's sense of peace and create an atmosphere conducive to thought. In addition to putting the observer in the right frame of mind, the Oriental water feature is intended to guide the visitor through the garden by linking together its various parts. As in the natural world, the garden should hold mysteries which are unraveled slowly as the path of the winding stream is followed. Water, rocks and plants are elaborately arranged into what amounts to a real life representation of a landscape painting.

In reality in the domestic garden, the best visual parts of the Oriental theme are often appropriated and used, and then planted liberally with appropriate Asian plants. The Oriental influence may extend no further than to a visual 'look.' The Japanese and Chinese passion for shaped rocks and raked gravel finds little favor in the West, but their overall designs for open water are proving to be increasingly popular.

Left: *A wonderful interpretation of an Oriental water garden. Peace and tranquillity pervade the atmosphere, helped immeasurably by the presence of water. The bamboo* shishi-odoshi *in the background with its gentle splash of water brings a little natural sound to the scene.*

formal planted pools

A formal pool can be planted as liberally as an informal one and look very fine, but for most gardeners the purpose of having a formal water feature is to enjoy the water in its own right, as much the prospect of cultivating aquatic plants. So the planting arrangements of formal pools are generally more restrained and often very symmetrical. Consideration is rarely given to creating a natural eco-balance in the pool, since it is difficult to produce a formal effect that is pleasing to the eye and at the same time have all the plant components necessary to ensure a balanced ecology.

Submerged plants are not essential to the well-being of a pool that is being managed artificially by chemicals, but they do make a major contribution. They produce life-giving oxygen and mop up excessive nutrients, thereby depriving suspended algae of a livelihood.

Floating plants, so popular in informal arrangements, find little favor with formal plantings. Surface leaf forms and blossoms are mostly provided by waterlilies or other deep-water aquatics such as water hawthorn, *Aponogeton distachyos*. However, when there is moving water, especially the splash of a fountain, then few deep-water aquatics, except the rather vulgar yellow pondlily, *Nuphar lutea*, will prosper.

Marginal aquatics are widely used for formal arrangements, especially reeds and rushes, although strong foliage plants like cannas and pontederia are excellent for focal plantings. All aquatic plants are best grown in planting baskets. Not only is this practical and functional, but it ensures that the plants remain precisely where they should and do not 'wander off' and spoil the carefully contrived visual effect.

Below: *There is no reason why a formal pool cannot be heavily planted if the distinct outlines of the feature remain clearly visible. The use of architectural plants with formal foliage can greatly enhance the overall appearance of the feature.*

Right: *Formality on a grand scale. The pool, arbor and lawned areas are all beautifully in proportion with one another. While the pool has clearly been placed to provide a reflection of the building, the water surface is not unduly cluttered by the clumps of waterlilies. The marginal plants in each corner of the pool both add to the formality and soften the paved edges.*

plants for formal features

There are an enormous number of aquatic plants which can be used effectively in formal ponds. These are mainly plants which give the features a particular theme or ambiance, although those that are purely practical should not be overlooked. Submerged plants can make an important contribution to the well-being of the ecology of the smaller pool, although visually they are of no significance. Choose species which rarely punctuate the water surface; those like *Elodea canadensis* are preferable when the glassy mirror-like stillness of the pool is of great importance. Lovely though they are, free-flowering submerged plants which raise their blossoms above the water, such as the water crowfoot, *Ranunculus aquatilis*, and water violet, *Hottonia palustris,* can so easily detract from the desired effect.

Waterlilies are excellent plants for creating surface interest. These root into baskets in the lower reaches of the pool and then push up their floating leaves and blossoms. All are excellent, but be sure to choose varieties that are suitable for the depth of water in the pool. If the water is too deep they will struggle and leaf sparsely, but conversely if too shallow they will climb out of the water in an unruly lump.

It is the marginal plants that set off formal water features. Architectural plants of easy-going disposition like *Schoenoplectus lacustris* and its variegated leafed cousin, the zebra rush, can be used to add a vertical note to the feature. The pickerel, *Pontederia cordata,* is a stately foliage plant and lovely when in flower, as are the recently introduced aquatic cannas known as 'Longwood Hybrids.'

CROSS-SECTION OF A POND SHOWING PLANTING DEPTHS

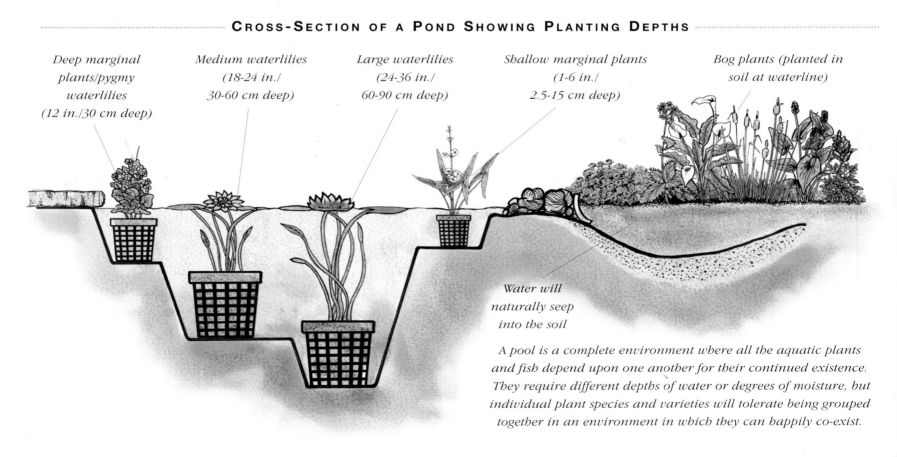

Deep marginal plants/pygmy waterlilies (12 in./30 cm deep)

Medium waterlilies (18-24 in./ 30-60 cm deep)

Large waterlilies (24-36 in./ 60-90 cm deep)

Shallow marginal plants (1-6 in./ 2.5-15 cm deep)

Bog plants (planted in soil at waterline)

Water will naturally seep into the soil

A pool is a complete environment where all the aquatic plants and fish depend upon one another for their continued existence. They require different depths of water or degrees of moisture, but individual plant species and varieties will tolerate being grouped together in an environment in which they can happily co-exist.

RECOMMENDED PLANT LIST

Waterlilies	*Flowering period*	*Color*	*Depth*	*Spread*
Nymphaea 'Ellisiana'	Summer	Red	16-24 in. (40-60 cm)	2-3 ft. (60-90 cm)
N. 'Froebeli'	Summer	Blood-red	16-24 in. (40-60 cm)	2-3 ft. (60-90 cm)
N. 'Gonnère'	Summer	White, double	18-36 in. (45-90 cm)	2-3 ft. (60-90 cm)
N. 'Marliacea Albida'	Summer	White	18-36 in. (45-90 cm)	2-4 ft. (60 cm-1.2 m)
N. 'Marliacea Chromatella'	Summer	Yellow, mottled foliage	18-36 in. (45-90 cm)	2-4 ft. (60 cm-1.2 m)
N. 'Pink Sensation'	Summer	Pink	18-36 in. (45-90 cm)	2-3 ft. (60-90 cm)
N. 'Rose Arey'	Summer	Pink, fragrant	18-30 in. (45-75 cm)	2-3 ft. (60-90 cm)

Deep-Water Aquatic	*Flowering period*	*Color*	*Depth*	*Spread*
Aponogeton distachyos	Summer	White, fragrant	12-36 in. (30-90 cm)	2-3 ft. (60-90 cm)

Marginal Plants	*Flowering period*	*Color*	*Depth*	*Spread*
Caltha palustris	Spring	Yellow	12-24 in. (30-60 cm)	1-2 ft. (30-60 cm)
Iris laevigata	Summer	Blue	24-36 in. (60-90 cm)	1-1½ ft. (30-45 cm)
Pontederia cordata	Summer	Blue	24-36 in. (60-90 cm)	1-1½ ft. (30-45 cm)
Schoenoplectus lacustris	Summer	Dark green foliage	24-36 in. (60-90 cm)	1-1½ ft. (30-45 cm)
Typha minima	Summer	Brown poker	18 in. (45 cm)	1 ft. (30 cm)

Submerged Aquatics	*Flowering period*	*Color*	*Depth*
Elodea canadensis	Semi-evergreen foliage	Dark green	6 in.-5 ft. (15 cm-1.5 m)
Myriophyllum aquaticum	Finely cut foliage	Blue-green	1-3 ft. (30-90 cm)
Potamogeton crispus	Crispy translucent foliage	Bronze-green	6 in.-40 in. (15 cm-1 m)

Bog Garden Plants	*Flowering period*	*Color*	*Depth*	*Spread*
Astilbe 'White Gloria'	Summer	White plumes	24-30 in. (60-75 cm)	1½-2 ft. (45-60 cm)
Hosta undulata 'Albomarginata'	Summer	Lilac/foliage variegated	24-30 in. (60 cm)	1½-2 ft. (45-60 cm)
Iris ensata	Summer	Deep purple	24-30 in. (60-75 cm)	1½-2 ft. (45-60 cm)
Primula aurantiaca	Early summer	Orange	24-36 in. (60-90 cm)	1½-2 ft. (45-60 cm)
Primula pulverulenta	Early summer	Deep red	24-36 in. (60-90 cm)	1½-2 ft. (45-60 cm)
Rheum palmatum	Summer	Cream/ handsome foliage	5-6 ft. (1.5-1.8 m)	3-5 ft. (1-1.5 m)

edging with stone and brick

The edge of the formal pond is usually easier to deal with than that of the informal pool, since a very definite line of hard landscaping is desirable to help delineate the formal shape of the pool. Stone, paving and bricks can all play a part in providing a suitable edge, but it should be remembered that such an edging is not only ornamental, but functional as well. It must be safe to walk on at any point, since formal pools by their very nature are uncluttered. And when edged with paving or bricks, they invite the visitor to dwell at the edge.

There are a wide range of hard landscape edging materials that can be used, but paving stones are the most popular. These are available in a variety of colors, sizes and finishes. From a visual viewpoint it is important to select a size that rests easily with the surface area of the pool. Large paving stones around a small pool rarely provide a pleasing arrangement, while small ones in a single row around a large expanse of water do little to enhance it. However, several rows of smaller pavers in a patterned arrangement can be very satisfactory visually.

Bricks and paving stones must all be fixed securely on a generous mortar bed. The mortar should not go right to the water's edge as spillage into the pool results in the release of harmful free-lime and the pond will need to be emptied and cleaned before stocking can take place. However, the mortar should be sufficient to secure the bricks or paving stones, which ideally should protrude just over the edge of the pool. This not only creates a much neater finish than when they are aligned directly with the wall of the pool, but, in a lined pool, it gives some measure of protection to the liner from the bleaching effect of the sun beating down on it above the waterline.

MAKING A STONE-PAVED EDGE

1 *Mark the edge of the pool with an edging iron. This should correspond with the outer edge of the paving stone when in its final position.*

2 *Remove a strip of turf or the soil up to the back edge. Allow a retaining lip of undisturbed soil to remain next to the water's edge.*

3 *Pull the liner and pool underlay tightly over the lip and back over the excavation and secure it in position in readiness for the mortar.*

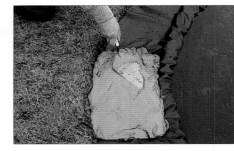

4 *Fill the excavated area with mortar. Extend this up to the lip, but not over it. The lip serves to prevent mortar spillage into the pond.*

5 *Carefully position the slabs. Curved slabs fit a round pool most easily, but you can create an attractive feature with oblong ones.*

6 *Work around the circumference of the pool, firming each slab in place as you go. Check the levels regularly – poolside paving must be level.*

Above: *A circular pool beautifully edged with paving slabs. Here pebbles have been set in concrete in a ring outside the slabs for wholly decorative effect. The planting softens the outer reaches of the feature.*

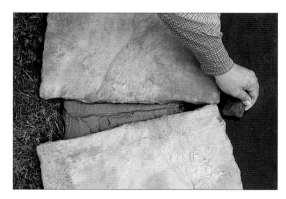

7 *Put a small piece of card beneath the gap at the poolside to prevent mortar spillage.*

8 *Put mortar between the paving slabs and add selected pebbles for decorative effect.*

9 *Once the mortar has dried out, remove the card shuttering from beneath the slabs.*

the natural look

Many gardeners want their ponds to have a natural appearance. The dream of the uninitiated is to have a natural soil-bottomed pond where the plants all grow with unrestrained abandon. It is a romantic notion, but one that usually becomes a nightmare, for rarely are truly natural ponds securely water-tight, and when given the luxury of unrestricted root-run most aquatic plants spread out of control. The secret to a successful natural-looking water garden is to create the appearance of nature but to use durable pond construction materials and to select less invasive plants of appropriate appearance for effect. Grow these within the restriction of containers.

It is possible to create a completely natural structure using a bentonite blanket or by mixing bentonite powder into clay loam soil in order to produce a seal, but pond liners and preformed ponds are much more secure options. Likewise the growing of plants in containers is the best way of exercising some control over them and producing the desired visual effect.

Just because a water garden is natural, it does not mean that it should only host native plants. Excellent natural effects can be created by the thoughtful arrangement of foreign species and garden varieties. It is true that such a mixture may not attract a wide variety of wildlife, but garden varieties of many plants hold some attraction for insects and butterflies.

Frogs, toads and other amphibians show little concern for the planting arrangement when they choose to colonize the pond, and providing suitable allowance is made for access to the shallows through the creation of a beach or shallow marginal shelf, birds of all kinds will be attracted to the pool to drink and bathe in the water.

Healthy plants help to establish a balanced eco-system.

lakes and open water

The large natural pond or lake is one of nature's wonders. If an existing body of natural water can be incorporated into the garden and enhanced, then the water gardener has the most perfect canvas upon which to paint a picture. Providing that the lake or large pond retains water at a consistent level all the year round, management is relatively simple and the feature remains visually appealing.

In many cases lakes and large ponds have to be created. The advantage of producing your own is that its depth and shape can be predetermined and accommodation made for planting to the desired effect. While such an enterprise requires careful planning, it produces additional opportunities for enhancing the garden landscape by the thoughtful redistribution of soil.

Indeed, where a large body of water is being produced artificially, it is wise to take into account the surrounding garden, even when you are working on a grand scale. The effect of a substantial stretch of water which is introduced into a hitherto featureless landscape can be remarkably dramatic, not just by its physical presence but also because of the pictures that it creates through reflections.

It is the latter aspect that can be the most visually arresting element, but often the wonderful pictures

produced by nearby trees, buildings or the scudding of fluffy white clouds across a bright blue sky are overlooked in the planning stage. The effects of the changing seasons must also be taken into account. The

dramatic transformation of a large body of water from a still azure blue mirror in summer to the gloomy gray and choppy surface of windswept winter will have a profound effect on the garden landscape.

Right: A beautifully planted large water garden. Marginal aquatics throng the waterside while clusters of well-maintained waterlilies provide a central focus.

Above: A lake that does not depend upon aquatic plants for its beauty. The reflections in the water are the main attraction.

Right: A large natural pond in a garden setting that has been enhanced by the careful management of the surrounding land.

informal garden ponds

The informal pond is great fun for the ardent gardener, for here almost anything goes and a wide variety of plants can be grown without too much consideration for overall visual appearance and symmetry. Most informal ponds reflect nature with regard to their shape and configuration, and planting consists of a tangled informality. They tend to be irregular in shape but they remain evidently part of the garden construct through the explicit use of hard edging, paving surrounds and the like. In this they differ from

Below: Tangled informality as plants throng the waterside. Order is brought by the manicured grass edge and the clear open water.

natural garden ponds (pages 88-89), which strive to mimic the look of a natural body of water even though they are artificially made.

While such a pond would appear to be very easily maintained, the reality is that considerable care has to be taken over planning and planting in order to produce the casual informal look. Maintenance also has to be both thorough and regular. The end result is well worthwhile, for of all water features the informal garden pond provides the greatest opportunity not only for enjoying plants and fish, but also for creating a whole self-sustaining watery eco-system.

Just as planting has to be carefully contrived in order to look natural, so too does the pool itself. There is a temptation to produce an intricate mathematical masterpiece with all kinds of fussy niches and contortions. However, such creations are not only a nightmare to construct, but they can be very tiresome to care for. The best informal ponds rely upon sweeping arcs and curves and depend much more upon thoughtful planting for producing the desired effect, although a stone or paved edge assists greatly in defining the pond in its setting.

Left: A pool that gives the enthusiastic gardener the opportunity to grow an extensive range of plants. The marginal aquatics are cleverly contained between stones, which form a hard decorative edge. Soil sculpting in the center permits the unfettered growth of waterlilies without incursions from marginal plants.

natural garden ponds

Unlike the informal garden pool, which – although planted in a naturalistic way – is clearly a part of the informal garden landscape, the natural pool brings the informality of the countryside into the garden while allowing you the luxury of eliminating weedy species of native origin in favor of more beautiful waterplants of your choice. The natural garden pond emulates the overall visual appearance of the pond found in the corner of the cow pasture with its clumps of reeds and floating waterlily pads, but it utilizes garden varieties of aquatics for

Above: A truly natural water garden has extensive moist margins where reeds, rushes and irises can prosper unhindered. Here a full range of bog and marginal aquatics throng the waterside in great profusion, but none of them advance too far into the pond.

landscape effect. Indeed, to the casual observer the pond and its plants appear to be natural phenomena caught in a garden setting.

The pond itself may be constructed in a traditional fashion, although the puddled clay of a hundred years ago has now been replaced by bentonite clay blankets or bentonite granules. These modern construction materials permit a very natural watertight clay finish to be applied to a pond excavation. Such a method of sealing the pond area is just about as close to nature as it is possible to get and opens up construction opportunities using clay, which

Left: There are few more attractive natural garden features than a waterside tangle of native bog and marginal aquatics mingled with wildflowers. They also attract a rich diversity of insects and birds.

Above: *A celebration of aquatic plants and water in a natural setting with adequate provision, in the shape of the bridge and pathway, for everyone to be able to enjoy it to the full.*

hitherto was a hazardous medium to use because of its propensity for leaking.

Not that the construction has to use natural materials. A pond liner or even a preformed pool can be the basis of a natural water garden if the edges are disguised carefully.

The use of heavy marginal planting which spills over onto surrounding ground is the easiest way of producing the natural look, although allowing grass to grow over the poolside also has its visual merits. Maintenance can be rather tedious, however, for grass requires regular clipping and this can be difficult to do without the cuttings dropping into the water. If such a problem can be overcome, then visually there are enormous benefits in such a method of edging.

installing a rigid pond

Rigid ponds are very convenient for water garden construction for all the levels are predetermined and the pond shell is watertight. However, as with all ponds, a little thought is necessary before installation, especially with regard to the lie of the land. It is imperative that when the pond is in its final position it is level from side to side and end to end, or else there will be flooding to one side and exposure of the pool wall at the other. Provision should be made for the soil surface to be level before the work of excavation commences.

Once this is achieved, the excavation can be created to suit the shape and size of the pond. Do not try to make it exactly the same size, but allow a little leeway so that when the pool is placed in position small adjustments can be made. This also means that there is room to introduce a cushioning layer of sand and adequate space for backfilling.

When the pool has been positioned correctly and backfilled with sand, check one more time that the levels are correct. The paved edging can then be added. A shallow excavation will be necessary around the edge of the pond to accommodate the thickness of the paving and a shallow mortar bed in which to set it in order to make it secure. This will ensure that the edging and the surrounding grass are level. Raised pond edgings in association with manicured grass create maintenance problems.

1 *Spread sand carefully and accurately around the base of the pool to mark out the shape. Remove the pool shell before digging commences.*

2 *Excavate to the depth of the marginal shelves. Add 2 in. (5 cm) all around to allow for the tapered shape.*

INSTALLING A RIGID POOL

Below: *The carefully arranged edging stones and imaginative waterside planting hide the fact that this is a rigid preformed pool.*

4 *Excavate the entire area. Remove an extra 2 in. (5 cm) of soil to allow for a sand base and backfill.*

5 *Remove any sharp stones from the hole. Then cover the shelves with a 2 in. (5 cm) layer of building sand.*

6 *Carefully lower the pool shell into the excavation. Make sure that it is sitting evenly on the sand bed.*

7 *With the pool in position, take a board and spirit level and adjust the pool as necessary to ensure that it is level from side to side and end to end.*

8 *Backfill with sand. This will flow evenly around the shell and support it.*

3 *Place the pond in the hole and mark around the outer edge with sand. This is a guide for the final excavation.*

9 *Once the pool has been installed, excavate around the edge so that a base can be laid for paving.*

10 *Paving is laid onto a layer of mortar on a shallow concrete base. The paving should slightly overhang the edge of the pool to disguise it.*

installing a pump and filter

When installing any filter, other than a straightforward physical or multi-purpose filter that sits within the pond, it is sensible to accommodate it separately to the side of the pond. More complex filters will require regular supervision and maintenance that can be best managed in a separate chamber and connected to the pump that operates within the pond.

Take care to ensure that the pump is powerful enough to operate the filter and any feature where water is to be moved. It is always wise to purchase a pump that has 25 per cent more capacity than is required. It can always be controlled downwards.

Situate the pump within the pond either on the flat bottom or on a suitable plinth. It is important that the pump is level and stable and that it can be easily retrieved from the side of the pond for cleaning and maintenance on a regular basis. In the set-up illustrated here, the outfall side of the pump discharges clean water back into the pond through a decorative fountain, while the input element draws dirty water through the pump to the combined bio-filter and UV sterilizer system. Modern pumps connect simply to filters and fountainheads by means of flexible hosing and stainless steel clips.

Apart from the volume of water necessary to operate any decorative feature, it is also important to consider any lift involved. Remember that the pump is likely to be on the bottom, or quite close to the bottom, of the pond and the outfall from an ornament may be 3 ft. (1 meter) or more above the surface of the water. To assist with this place the pump as close to the outfall as possible. Initially adjustments will have to be made to the pump until the correct water flow is established and to ensure that there is no wasteful splashing.

COMBINED BIOFILTER AND UV STERILIZER

Water is pumped from the pond into the filter and is forced through a foam block, which extracts floating particles. The bacteria colonizing the foam convert toxic waste products into nutrients, which are available to the plants. The clean water then passes a UV bulb that kills off any algae and parasites.

Unit housing ultra-violet (UV) bulb and electrical connections to run it

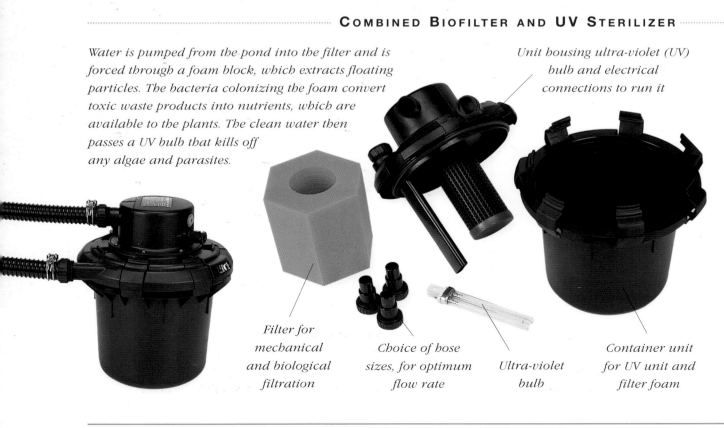

Filter for mechanical and biological filtration

Choice of hose sizes, for optimum flow rate

Ultra-violet bulb

Container unit for UV unit and filter foam

Above: *The biofilter can be accommodated in a concrete collar situated beneath the paving at the poolside.*

INSTALLING A SUBMERSIBLE PUMP

1 *Assemble the fountainhead and T-piece. Connect the hose using the largest diameter flexible hose that will fit the pump.*

2 *Tighten up the hose clip so that it does not slip. Do not over-tighten as the fountainhead connection may crack.*

3 *Push the T-piece onto the pump outlet. An extension tube can be fitted to lift the fountainhead to the desired height.*

4 *The fountain regulator valve also controls the water flow to the filter. As the fountain flow is increased, the filter flow lessens.*

5 *Position the pump in the pond before connecting to the electricity supply. Connect the hose running from the pump to the inlet on the filter.*

6 *The return pipe taking water from the filter to the pond can be disguised by connecting it to an ornament, here a decorative fish. The pipes can be hidden away beneath the paving slabs.*

Above: Once the water is running, check that the flow rate through the filter is sufficient for correct functioning. To work out the flow rate, time how long it takes to fill a 2½ gallon (10 liter) bucket.

making a lined pool

Making a pool with a liner is probably the most popular construction method. As with a preformed pool, it is essential from the beginning to ensure that the site is level so that when water is added to the pool it does not flood out of one end. Such an error is difficult to rectify once a liner is installed.

Creating the shape of the pool is best achieved by using a length of hosepipe or rope to delineate its shape. This allows you to assess the overall look and proportion of the pool before you start to dig. Spread the hosepipe out on the ground to form the outline of the pool surface. It can be easily adjusted at this stage to produce exactly what is required. Fussy corners are generally not desirable as they present difficulties when it comes to putting in the liner and producing a crease-free finish.

A lined pool takes the shape of the final excavation. Shelves and levels are created solely from the soil profile. Thus, undisturbed ground is ideal for pool excavation. Previously cultivated soil can present difficulties and the collapsing of the pool profile can easily occur. This is also a problem on stony land where the soil structure is unstable. In such circumstances the installation of a preformed pond is to be preferred.

Stones can also be troublesome in a clay or loam soil, especially if they are near the surface, since water pressure within the liner can sometimes lead to puncturing as the stones are forced into the liner. To avoid this an underlay should be used. It is put into the excavation and dampened so that it clings to the walls. The liner is then spread over this and the pool filled with water. As water is added, the liner should be smoothed out by hand. Creases are best removed as the pool fills, as they are impossible to deal with later.

Finally the edges of the liner are tucked beneath the turf, if you plan a natural planted look, or trapped beneath stones or paving in a semi-formal situation.

MAKING A LINED POOL

1 *Mark out the area of the intended excavation with a length of garden hose. Ensure that the curves are smooth.*

2 *Excavate the pool to the depth of the shelves. These should be deep enough to accommodate a planting basket.*

3 *Excavate the full depth of the pool, digging down from the marginal shelves to create the deepest central pool.*

4 *Level off the floor of the hole using a mattock. Remove any stones or other sharp objects that may puncture the liner.*

5 *Ensure that the marginal shelves as well as the edges of the pool are level from side to side and end to end.*

6 *Place protective underlay into the excavation, molding it to the shape of the hole. This serves as a cushion for the liner.*

7 *Dampen the underlay so that it clings accurately to the shape of the excavation. This makes it easier to install the liner.*

8 *Spread the liner out and try to mold it to the contours of the hole. Make sure to allow sufficient overlap all around.*

9 *Remove as many creases as possible, working from the bottom up. It helps if the liner has been warmed by the sun.*

10 *Add water from a garden hose. As the water rises and presses against the walls of the pool, smooth out the creases.*

11 *The pool is complete and ready for planting. The liner has been trimmed to shape and tucked under the grass at the edge of the pool. The stones placed around the edge help to hide the top of the pool liner from view along the margin of the shelves.*

Above: *Thoughtful planting not only hides the edge of the liner, but successfully unites the water with the surrounding garden landscape. Marginal aquatics can disguise the edge from within the pool, waterside plants by tumbling over the edge.*

bog gardens

The bog garden is a valuable adjunct to the water garden, providing opportunities for growing moisture-loving plants that cannot be successfully cultivated in the margins of the pond itself. These are plants that find ordinary herbaceous border conditions too dry and hostile, although a number of them, like astilbes and hostas, are often established in the open garden.

Apart from offering the keen gardener a perfect place for indulging a passion for plants that are difficult to grow elsewhere, the bog garden is a visually appealing addition to the natural water garden, although it does not necessarily have to be an integral part of such a feature. Wonderful bog gardens can be created as completely separate garden features and designed in either an informal or formal fashion.

The main requirement for a bog garden is consistent moisture. While really wet conditions can usually be tolerated during the summer months, when winter arrives the soil should be no more than very damp. There should certainly never be water standing on the surface. When a bog garden stands adjacent to a pond, then the water level and moisture content of the bog area can be more easily regulated than if the feature is in isolation and separated

from the surrounding soil by a waterproof membrane.

Successful bog gardens also extend the flowering season at the waterside, since there are several bog plants that start flowering in very early spring and others which continue the season beyond the time when waterlilies and marginals are in flower. Some others have colorful autumn foliage.

Above: A well-planted bog garden, in which the upright sword-like foliage of the irises and feathery fronds of the ostrich feather ferns provide summer-long interest.

Left: Candelabra primulas, such as Primula pulverulenta, *are part of the backbone of the late spring- and early summer-flowering bog garden. Primulas are among those bog garden plants which offer the longest flowering period.*

Above: A bog garden should ideally be a natural adjunct to a pond, the water from the pool dampening the soil and helping to sustain the plants.

constructing a bog garden

A bog garden can either be an integral part of the water garden or an independent feature in its own right. When sited adjacent to a pond, it is quite simple to use the water in the pond to maintain a suitable level of moisture in the soil by creating a permeable membrane between the two. If the bog garden is to be completely independent, then other arrangements have to be made to ensure constant moisture; otherwise it becomes isolated from the surrounding garden and can in fact turn out to be a drier and more hostile environment for plants.

The construction of a bog garden is similar to that of a lined pool, except that there are no variable depths and the overall excavation need be no more than 18 in. (45 cm). Thus it is a shallow basin that is lined either with a pool liner or plain builders' polyethylene. As the lining is completely disguised and there is no direct contact with sunlight, which can degrade polyethylene, any cheap waterproof material can be used.

Once the liner is installed, the base should be pricked with a fork to allow excess water to drain away during winter. A bog garden that has standing water on the surface at any time of the year is likely to be a failure. A layer of gravel is added so that the holes will not become sealed by the heavy organic soil that bog garden plants so enjoy.

While watering a free-standing bog garden regularly is one way of ensuring plenty of moisture, the opportunity can alternatively be taken of adding a seep irrigation hose at the stage just before the soil is added during construction. This can be very discreetly introduced and it will not not visible after planting has been completed.

Above: *A bog garden is an attractive addition to a pool or stream. A wide range of moisture-loving plants produce interest from early spring until autumn.*

BOG GARDEN CONSTRUCTION

1 *Here the liner for the bog garden is being tacked to a timber frame with felt nails.*

2 *With the liner in place, a fork is used to puncture it to provide some drainage holes.*

3 *A generous layer of gravel is raked over the floor of the bog garden to assist drainage.*

4 *Irrigation hose is put in place so that, when construction is complete, the moisture level can be controlled.*

5 *A richly organic soil is ideal for a bog garden. This is raked out evenly in a thick layer over the gravel.*

6 *The planting of pot-grown plants can take place at any time of the year. In the summer months they must be well watered until established.*

7 *Allow sufficient space between the plants so that they can develop fully and for ease of maintenance.*

PLANTING SUGGESTIONS

Plants Used

Aruncus sylvester 'Kneiffii'/summer/bog

Astilbe taquettii 'Superba'/summer/bog

Hemerocallis 'Black Knight'/summer/bog

Hosta tardiana/summer/bog

Lysimachia nummularia 'Goldii'/summer/bog

Lysimachia punctata 'Alexander'/summer/bog

Monarda didyma 'Petite Delight'/summer/bog

Onoclea sensibilis/spring/summer/bog

Primula florindae/summer/bog

Zantedeschia aethiopica 'Crowborough'/
summer/bog

Alternative Plants

Iris sibirica/summer/bog

Ligularia hybrids/late summer/bog

Lobelia vedrariensis/late summer/bog

Rodgersia aesculifolia/summer/bog

Below: *An attractively planted bog garden with a rich diversity of colorful moisture-loving plants. Foliage color and form are an added bonus throughout the season.*

wildlife ponds

Wildlife ponds take many and varied forms, but in all cases the pond exists as a magnet for wildlife and a resource which the local fauna can enjoy. There are, for example, dewponds which scarcely support any plants in nature but provide watering holes for animals. When re-created and clay-lined in a garden setting, they can offer some accommodation for plants. Then there are ponds with varying depths for planting which are soil-sculpted to produce open water and a balanced eco-system, and shallow water bodies which are heavily planted and have little exposed water, but myriad wildlife. The latter are the most interesting to observe, but they are difficult to maintain in good order while retaining their tangled countryside character.

A wildlife pond can develop from virtually any pond, for within days of construction and water being added, the first aquatic insect life will arrive without any further encouragement. When plants are added, more populations will appear quite naturally. However, to create a pond where wildlife is the focus, plant selection should be of species and varieties that attract interesting insects and birds. For the most part these should be native plants, for there is a greater chance of wildlife diversity establishing if natural host and food plants are introduced, although

Below: The marsh marigold, Caltha palustris, *is one of the finest harbingers of spring and a valuable addition to the wildlife pool.*

these are often not the most colorful and interesting from a garden decoration point of view.

Choosing plants which have potential for food and shelter is important for creating opportunities for predators to prey upon creatures which are attracted to the plants. Sympathetic pond construction, perhaps by including a cobbled beach or an island, also adds greatly to the likelihood of wildlife visiting the pool and helps an ecologically balanced environment to become quickly established.

Above: *When there is sufficient plant cover, frogs and toads invariably arrive. They capture and eat a wide variety of insects as well as slugs and snails.*

Left: *A wonderful diversity of bog, marginal and moisture-loving plants. Included are* Pontederia cordata *'Alba,'* Carex, Ranunculus *and* Physostegia virginiana. *All provide cover or sustenance for aquatic insect life.*

making a wildlife pool

Wildlife gardening aims to create places where animals and plants can thrive alongside humans in the domestic environment. A wildlife pool is normally constructed in the same way as a conventional garden pool, especially if the creation of a balanced eco-system is an objective. However, a layer of soil can be included on top of the liner so that plants can root directly into the soil rather than being confined in planting baskets as is often the case with conventional lined ponds.

The various depths of water necessary for the successful establishment of plants that will produce a balanced eco-system are essential. Marginal shelves should be provided to accommodate marginal aquatics, and deep water between 18 in. (45 cm) and 3 ft. (90 cm) in depth is needed for waterlilies, other deep-water aquatics and submerged plants, along with sufficient surface area for the free exchange of gases and the establishment of floating plants. Such conditions also provide all that is necessary for fish, snails and amphibians.

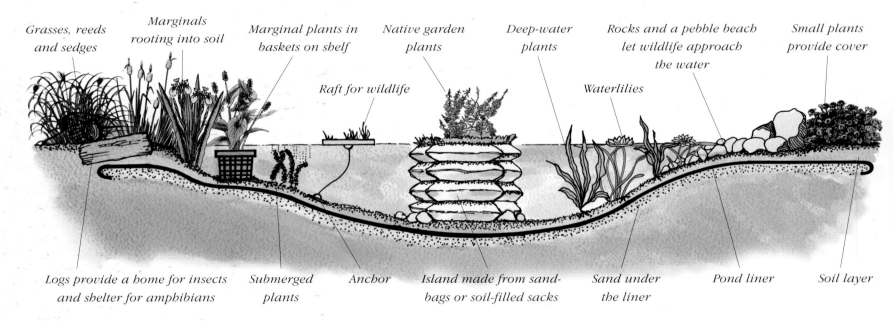

Grasses, reeds and sedges

Marginals rooting into soil

Marginal plants in baskets on shelf

Native garden plants

Deep-water plants

Rocks and a pebble beach let wildlife approach the water

Small plants provide cover

Raft for wildlife

Waterlilies

Logs provide a home for insects and shelter for amphibians

Submerged plants

Anchor

Island made from sand-bags or soil-filled sacks

Sand under the liner

Pond liner

Soil layer

MAKING A BEACH

1 *The addition of a beach extension to a lined pool is simple if done at the time of construction. Rake out soil from the excavation from intended water level to the bank.*

2 *Cut the underlay and spread it out from below the water level to the edge of the beach. Dampen it with water to assist with laying and cut off excess.*

The way in which construction is undertaken often differs from that of a decorative garden pool, for unlike the order required in the garden, one of the main attractions of a wildlife pool is the tangled growth of the often ungainly native species. So planting baskets are often abandoned and the plants permitted to find their place in the pool. If not controlled a number of the popular weedy species will invade the entire pool. Rather than wait for this to occur, create a pool with a profile that will prevent this happening. Where areas of open water are desired, sculpt the profile so that at the edge of the desired planted area the water depth exceeds 18 in. (45 cm). Very few marginal species will tolerate this and are naturally root pruned where the water becomes deeper.

A wildlife pool is not only about aquatic inhabitants and insect life. There are many birds which can be enjoyed at the pool side if provision is made for them. If a beach is constructed, then they can walk into the water and drink, and they will also greatly enjoy the opportunity of bathing in the margins. A simple wooden ramp also allows small mammals and amphibians easy access to the water.

Right: A wildlife pond that includes a wide variety of worthy aquatic plants. Such a feature, with a full complement of plants, is likely to retain a naturally sustainable eco-system. It is doubtless a haven for amphibians, birds and aquatic insect life.

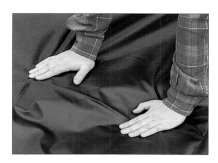

3 Mold the liner to the shape of the excavation, smoothing out as many creases as possible. If folds are necessary, make them simple and generous.

4 Tuck the liner under the turf, and, starting from the upper edge of the beach, use cobbles to create the surface. Use larger sizes at the top of the beach.

Right: The beach is complete. A beach gives birds an opportunity to drink and bathe. It also provides a simple exit for frogs and toads and an emergency exit for any adventurous hedgehogs.

making a clay-lined dewpond

In years gone by, many ponds around the country-side were lined with clay. This involved a complicated and time-consuming process called puddling. Where the soil was at least half clay by volume, pure clay, often of a blue gault kind, was brought in to produce a waterproof lining. Once the excavation had been prepared, it was dusted heavily with soot so that earthworms would be deterred from puncturing it once the clay was laid. The clay was mixed with water, much as a potter fashioning a pot might do, and it was then smeared on the walls of the excavation, starting at the bottom and working to the top. Once complete, the pool was filled with water.

Apart from being a dirty and labor-intensive method of construction, it always had a high maintenance requirement, for unless the clay between the surface of the surrounding ground and the surface of the water in the pond was regularly dampened, cracks would appear and the pond would start to leak. It was also vulnerable to penetration by the roots of nearby shrubs and trees.

Fortunately modern clay materials have overcome this, and with the introduction of purified bentonite

Left: Bentonite clay blanket is a remarkable product for lining a pool, for if punctured it is self-sealing. Here a knife has been thrust through the blanket to demonstrate its ability to seal itself around a puncture wound.

LINING A DEWPOND

1 *Mark out the area to be excavated. Use a line and two stakes to inscribe a circle.*

2 *Excavate the hole in the position to the required depth and remove the spoil.*

3 *Rake over the excavation and remove large stones. Create as even a surface as possible.*

4 *Unroll the blanket, ensuring that there is enough overlap at the pool edge.*

5 *Cut the bentonite blanket to size using a sharp knife. This pond requires two widths.*

6 *Fold back the top layer, and peel the geotextile covering from the lower one to expose the clay.*

7 *Flap the top layer down again so that the black textile makes contact with the clay.*

8 *Fold the geotextile back into place and pat the blanket firmly to make a secure joint.*

Above: *The blanket is made of a layer of clay trapped between two layers of geotextile fabric.*

9 *Once lined, water can be added. This changes the composition of the clay, which can be molded like Plasticine™. Firming down along the joint creates a seal.*

10 *The pond can then be filled. A thick layer of soil can be added if you want to add plants.*

11 *The edges of the bentonite blanket are then trimmed and neatly tucked beneath the turf.*

clay a similar effect can be achieved much more quickly and conveniently. Bentonite clay is a dry granular material which swells up when in contact with water and naturally seals the soil with which it is mixed, providing that this consists of at least half clay content. For large-scale ponds and lagoons this is ideal, but for the small pond it is not quite so easy to employ.

The alternative is the bentonite blanket that sandwiches a layer of bentonite clay between two layers of textile and which can be purchased in prepacked rolls. It is laid in the excavation in a similar manner to a pond liner. Individual lengths are joined together in a self-sealing way; the bentonite clay will bond to the adjacent sheet as illustrated. When water is added, the joins seal together to make a waterproof lining. Planting can be in containers, or a thick layer of soil can be added on top of the blanket into which plants can root directly. Pebbles can be used on top of this soil layer as a top dressing to create a more pleasing visual effect.

Above: *Dewponds are naturally occurring ponds which collect water from the surrounding land or are sometimes spring-fed. They are usually devoid of aquatic plants and serve as nature's mirrors, reflecting the sky and all about them.*

water meadows

Water meadows are naturally areas of land in river catchment areas that are periodically inundated with flood water. The water carries with it a rich silt which is deposited over the area, usually sparingly and rather like a fertilizer. Sometimes the river does not swamp the land completely, but the water table is so high that puddles form on the surface of the land and remain there for much of the winter.

Water meadows are noted for their lush grass – not usually of tussocky or vigorously running species, but some of the finer kinds. It is among such a sward that moisture-loving pasture plants like water aven, *Geum rivale*, globe flower, *Trollius europaeus*, and ragged robin, *Lychnis flos-cucculi*, prosper. A number of bulbs enjoy it too, notably the snakeshead fritillary, *Fritillaria meleagris* and the snowflake, *Leucojum aestivum*.

In a garden setting a water garden can be established as a lawned extension from the edge of the pond. It is best not to try to convert existing lawn to water meadow, but to set up a proper area, ideally using a fine grass seed mixture and inserting the young plants as plugs into emerging seedling turf in the spring. Some seed companies sell grass seed mixtures with the seeds of native water meadow plants included, but while success for the grass is more or less

assured, this cannot be guaranteed for the colorful flowering plants.

Maintenance of the water meadow is fairly simple. It cannot be treated like a lawn, for regular close mowing will cut out the plants and bulbs. The grass has to be allowed to grow for a sufficiently long period to permit seeding of the meadow plants and guarantee that the foliage of the bulbs has an opportunity to rebuild its strength. Such areas are treated much as those dedicated to naturalized bulbs and need minimal management.

Right: *A water meadow is a long-term project. Careful minimal management allows choice hardy moisture-loving orchids like* Dactylorhiza fuchsii *to get established.*

Above: *An area of water meadow, which has been enhanced by colorful planting of moisture-loving plants.*

Right: *Not all water meadows are restricted to native flora. Here a blend of good garden plants like* Hosta, Iris *and* Primula *mingle with native wetland species.*

edging an informal pond

The edge of a pool is important, since it defines the water body visually and also provides a secure place to stand and enjoy the fruits of one's labor. By carefully constructing the edge, the point where pool meets land can be a positive attribute of the feature. So often it is the transition from pool to garden that ruins the overall effect of a water feature.

Paving is one of the most popular forms of edging and, if laid properly, it is secure, good looking and maintenance-free. Whether the pool is of liner or preformed construction, the surrounding ground should be reduced by the combined depth of the proposed paving stone and mortar bed. This assumes that the edge of the pool is at the level of the bottom of the mortar base. If it is at ground level, then soil will need to be made up behind the paving.

There is a great diversity of paving materials available for the home gardener: not just square or rectangular slabs, but ones cut at an angle so that a curve can be easily achieved. When an informal pool is going to have some fairly eccentric curves and arcs, it is sensible to check the shapes of available slabs before deciding upon the shape of the pool.

Of course, if the pool already exists and the paving is a later addition, or you have a new pool but must use landscaping materials that match other garden features, cutting to shape may be necessary, a cold chisel being the best tool for the job. Paving is laid on a generous bed of mortar, each slab protruding slightly over the edge of the pool to assist in its disguise. Each slab should be level and the gap between be pointed with mortar.

Not all edging has to use hard materials – an informal pool looks very effective with grass running up to the water. While this can be quite natural, with the pool liner tucked under the existing turf, another option is to establish turf on a layer of rock wool (a type of building insulation material). This can be brought right to the edge of the water and consolidated over the liner.

EDGING A POND

1 *It is important to lay paving stones on a firm base. Make a concrete mix with coarse builders' sand and cement, six parts to one by volume. Mix with water until a sticky agglomeration.*

2 *Excavate the soil around the pool edge so that the concrete base can be spread. The slabs are usually laid on a mortar bed comprising three parts by volume bricklayer's sand and one part cement.*

3 *At one point in the paving insert a short length of plastic pipe between the paving slabs. This will permit access for an electrical cable if a pump or lights are to be installed later.*

4 Mortar is spread out with a trowel, taking care not to let it drop in the water. It should be about 1 in. (2.5 cm) deep.

5 Ensure that the paving slabs are level and also provide a small overhang at the edge.

6 If the paving slabs are a little high they can be gently tamped down by tapping them with the handle of a lump hammer.

7 Occasionally it may be necessary to cut a paving slab. This is best done on a soft base using a hammer and cold chisel.

8 The paved edging is nearing completion. The overhang provided by the paving slabs hides the liner.

9 Cut slabs should be used to ensure that the paved edge has a neat outline. Carefully bed them into the mortar.

10 Point the joints between the paving slabs with mortar. This not only provides a finish, but also secures them.

11 Dragging an old metal bucket handle or piece of pipe along the joints can neatly finish the surface of the mortar.

Above: The paved edge makes a secure, neat finish and also provides a visual frame for the in-pool planting.

what plants where?

There are so many plants that can be used in a natural water garden, but if attracting wildlife is a main objective, it is usual to concentrate on native species, even if they are a little less showy. Plants from other countries and continents may prove to be a mecca for insects and birds, but the planting of native kinds always enhances the prospects for successful wildlife interaction.

Where wildlife is not a prime concern, but a rugged natural look is the objective, then it really does not matter what species or varieties are used. Their visual attributes are paramount, but they should still be introduced in a

MARGINAL PLANTS

Carex pendula (**pendulous sedge**)/brownish (also almost evergreen foliage)/summer Height 1½-2 ft. (45-60 cm). Spread 1½-2 ft. (45-60 cm). Depth up to 4 in. (10 cm).

Calla palustris (**bog arum**)/white/summer Height 6 in.-1 foot (15-30 cm). Spread 4-6 in. (10-15 cm). Depth up to 4 in. (10 cm).

Caltha palustris (**marsh marigold**)/yellow/spring Height 1-2 ft. (30-60 cm). Spread 4-6 in. (10-15 cm). Depth up to 1 foot (30 cm).

Iris laevigata/blue/summer Height 2-3 ft. (60-90 cm). Spread 1-1½ ft. (30-45 cm). Depth up to 6 in. (15 cm).

Iris pseudacorus/yellow/summer Height 3-4 ft. (90 cm-1.2 m). Spread 1½-2 ft. (45-60 cm). Depth up to 10 in. (25 cm).

Lysimachia nummularia/yellow/summer Height 1 inch (2.5 cm). Spread 1-1½ ft. (30-45 cm). Depth up to 4 in. (10 cm).

Myosotis scorpiodies (**water forget-me-not**)/blue/summer Height 8-10 in. (20-25 cm). Spread 4-6 in. (10-15 cm). Depth up to 4 in. (10 cm).

Pontederia cordata (**pickerel**)/blue/late summer Height 2-3 ft. (60-90 cm). Spread 1-1½ ft. (30-45 cm). Depth up to 6 in. (15 cm).

Typha minima (**dwarf Japanese bulrush**)/brown fruiting heads/autumn Height 18 in. (45 cm). Spread 6-8 in. (15-20 cm). Depth up to 4 in. (10 cm).

Veronica beccabunga (**brooklime**)/dark blue/summer Height 6-8 in. (15-20 cm). Spread 4 in. (10 cm). Depth up to 4 in. (10 cm).

SUBMERGED PLANTS

Height is not applicable to these plants and spread is unpredictable. They will tolerate water between 1-3 ft. (30-90 cm) in depth.

Elodea canadensis (**Canadian pondweed**)/evergreen foliage/all year round.

Hottonia palustris (**water violet**)/white lilac flowers/summer.

Myriophyllum proserpinacoides (**parrot's feather**)/finely cut blue-green foliage/spring/summer.

Ranunculus aquatilis (**water crowfoot**)/white-gold flowers/summer.

BOG GARDEN PLANTS

Astilbe arendsii **hybrids**/red, pink, white/summer Height 1½-2 ft. (45-90 cm). Spread 10 in.-1½ ft. (25-45 cm).

Cardamine pratensis (**cuckoo flower**)/rosy-lilac/spring Height 1-1½ ft. (30-45 cm). Spread 6-10 in. (15-25 cm).

Filipendula ulmaria (**meadowsweet**)/creamy-white/summer Height 2-4 ft. (60 cm-1.2 m). Spread 1-2 ft. (30-60 cm).

Hosta fortunei (**plantain lily**)/lilac/violet, grayish foliage/summer Height 2-3 ft. (60-90 cm). Spread 1-1½ ft. (30-45 cm).

Iris ensata/purple/summer Height 2-2½ ft. (60-75 cm). Spread 1-1½ ft. (30-45 cm).

Matteuccia struthiopteris (**ostrich feather fern**)/green foliage/summer Height 3 ft. (90 cm). Spread 1½ ft. (45 cm).

Primula candelabra **hybrids**/many colors/summer Height 2-2½ ft. (60-75 cm). Spread 1-1⅓ ft. (30-40 cm).

Rheum palmatum (**ornamental rhubarb**)/white/summer Height 5-6 ft. (1.5-1.8 m). Spread 2½-3 ft. (75-90 cm).

Zantedeschia aethiopica (**arum lily**)/white/summer Height 2-2½ ft. (60-75 cm). Spread 1-1½ ft. (30-45 cm).

manner which enables a natural eco-balance to be maintained, particularly within the water body.

Marginal aquatics provide much of the poolside decoration, but submerged aquatics are vital in mopping up excessive nutrients from the water where they encourage the development of water-discoloring algae, while floating plants and deep-water aquatics reduce light falling beneath the water and make it difficult for algae to become established.

Left: *For the best effect, bog plants like* Primula bulleyana *and* Zantedeschia aethiopica *should be planted in groups.*

Below: *The long lance-shaped leaves of* Hosta longissima *provide a perfect foil for the beautiful soft pink blossom of the waterlily.*

FLOATING PLANTS

These have negligible heights and spread is unpredictable. They will tolerate any depth of water over 6 in. (15 cm).

Hydrocharis morsus-ranae (frogbit)/white/summer.
Utricularia vulgaris (greater bladderwort)/yellow/summer.

DEEP-WATER AQUATICS

Aponogeton distachyos (water hawthorn)/white and black/late spring/autumn Spread 1-3 ft. (30-90 cm). Depth 1-3 ft. (30-90 cm).
Nuphar advena (American spatterdock)/yellow/summer Spread 1½-5 ft. (45 cm-1.5 m). Depth 1½-5 ft. (45 cm-1.5 m).
Nuphar lutea (yellow pond lily)/yellow/summer Spread 1-8 ft. (30 cm-2.4 m). Depth 1-8 ft. (30 cm-2.4 m).
Orontium aquaticum (golden club)/gold-white/summer Spread 1½ ft. (45 cm). Depth 1½ ft. (45 cm).

WATERLILIES (ALL FLOWER DURING SUMMER)

Nymphaea 'Arc-en-ciel'/pink with variegated foliage Spread 1½-3 ft. (45-90 cm). Depth 1½-3 ft. (45-90 cm).
Nymphaea 'Charles de Meurville'/plum-red Spread 4-6 ft. (1.2-1.8 m). Depth 4-6 ft. (1.2-1.8 m).
Nymphaea 'Escarboucle'/crimson Spread 1-2 ft. (30-60 cm). Depth 1-2 ft. (30-60 cm).
Nymphaea 'Hermine'/white Spread 1-2 ft. (30-60 cm). Depth 1-2 ft. (30-60 cm).
Nymphaea 'Gladstone'/white Spread 4-8 ft. (1.2-2.4 m). Depth 4-8 ft. (1.2-2.4 m).
Nymphaea 'Marliacea Albida'/white Spread 1½-3 ft. (45-90 cm). Depth 1½-3 ft. (45-90 cm).
Nymphaea 'Marliacea Carnea'/pink Spread 4-6 ft. (1.2-1.8 m). Depth 4-6 ft. (1.2-1.8 m).
Nymphaea 'Marliacea Chromatella'/yellow Spread 1½-2½ ft. (45-75 cm). Depth 1½-2½ ft. (45-75 cm).
Nymphaea 'Rose Arey'/pink Spread 1½-2½ ft. (45-75 cm). Depth 1½-2½ ft. (45-75 cm).
Nymphaea 'Gonnère'/white Spread 3-4 ft. (90 cm-1.2 m). Depth 3-4 ft. (90 cm-1.2 m).

introducing moving water to the garden

Moving water is a tremendous asset in the garden. Sparkling fountains, tumbling waterfalls, streams, rills and canals can add much to the pleasure derived from a water garden. Even small features can accommodate moving water. The development of the submersible pump into an easily concealed, compact powerhouse for moving water has revolutionized water gardening.

It is now possible to create a bubbling water feature in a large pot, an urn or a carefully positioned millstone. Waterfalls, cascades and chutes can all be serviced by the modern submersible pump, often from the same unit that is operating a fountain. By changing the head on the fountain outlet of the pump, it is possible to produce a foaming geyser, a spreading bell fountain or conventional spray arrangement. By using suitable lighting it is a simple matter to illuminate them at night.

Moving water is not just a visual phenomenon; it also brings sounds to the garden. A gentle tinkling of spray from a fountain, the splashing and tumbling of a stream over a cascade, and the gushing forth of white water from a geyser enchant the ear.

Not that this sound, movement and excitement is without cost, for by introducing moving water, limitations are brought to bear upon the range of plants that can be grown. Many lovely aquatics, like waterlilies, are plants of quiet backwaters. They resent moving water and deteriorate when subjected to it, so the introduction of moving water requires the gardener to weigh in the balance its undoubted merits against the restrictions that it places upon the plants that can be enjoyed.

Three foaming jets bring life to a simple formal pool.

natural waterfalls

There are few features in the garden more attractive than a natural waterfall, a gentle meander over water-worn stone into a pool alive with the bright colors of goldfish and framed by groups of reeds and rushes. Not only does this bring movement to the garden, but also it introduces magical sound and the opportunity to be really creative.

A natural waterfall is probably the most pleasing of all the waterfall and cascade systems available to the home gardener, but to get such a feature to appear as if plucked from nature and incorporated seamlessly into the garden requires skill and forethought. The topography of the

Below: A wonderful natural-looking waterfall created with local stone which is layered as if it has evolved over time.

garden is a major contributor to its success, for if there is a natural slope which forms part of the garden scene, incorporation of a waterfall into the landscape becomes quite natural. Where earth-moving has to be undertaken to create a suitable landfall, then considerable skill is required in sculpting the soil.

The choice of rocks is important, since to look natural they need to be of local origin, or else in keeping with the theme of the garden. The quality of stone must also be considered as some flake and shale during severe winter weather when constantly exposed to water. It is important that any stone used is from a reliable supplier who can attest to the fact that it is free from any conservation constraints. Nowadays there are a number of excellent artificial stones which are extremely difficult to distinguish from the real thing.

Plants are very important in dressing a natural waterfall. The choice is restricted a little as some species and varieties do not enjoy constant movement, but there are sufficient colorful and pleasing kinds both to soften the edges of the waterfall and to add a touch of spring and summer color.

Left: This traditional garden waterfall uses all elements to great advantage. It reflects the informality of the garden and, while obviously an artificial construct, the arrangement is very pleasing. Generous opportunities are available to enable planting to become established.

formal waterfalls

When constructing a natural waterfall there are all kinds of rules to obey if you want the feature to appear as if contrived by nature. With a formal waterfall imagination can have full run, not only with regard to the arrangement of the falls and curtains of water, but with materials as well. It is possible to use most hard materials ranging from stone, slate, concrete and glass to metal, tile and even wood. The opportunities for creative design are limitless.

One of the main considerations when creating a formal waterfall should be light. It is important for any plants that might be incorporated into the overall scheme, but it is fundamental to a pleasing visual outcome with moving water. The most inspired waterfall creation will look mundane unless the play of light is fully exploited.

Formal waterfalls that are of a preformed construction are the easiest to install and operate successfully. There is a uniformity that makes it simple from the outset to calculate water requirements, and often much of the mental endeavor is already done for you so that installation is much like building from a kit. The more imaginative formal arrangements demand deeper thought.

Indeed, with a unique formal waterfall, even when of very simple construction, thinking time is equally as important as construction time, since getting things wrong once the project is well under way can prove a nightmare. Serious problems usually only occur when ambition overtakes realism. If careful calculations are made regarding the spread of water and the flow required to create the desired curtain or fall, then the materials from which the feature is made are of secondary importance.

Left: *To create an even curtain of water, the lip of the cascade must be absolutely level and very smooth. Irregularities in the stone will create turbulence. Marginal aquatics provide an attractive dressing for the pool, but do not enjoy growing in the direct flow of the water.*

Above: *A startling cascade appearing from among a leafy plant at the end of a rill. A perfect curtain of water can only be achieved by using a sufficiently powerful pump to move a large volume of water.*

Opposite page: *A charming set of formal waterfalls which are accompanied by harmonious but informal plantings. It is important with such a feature to calculate drops and flow rates very carefully. A powerful pump will be required to produce the necessary lift.*

making a waterfall using liner

A pool liner offers the most flexible method of creating a waterfall or cascade. An excavation can be created and lined which reflects exactly the intentions of the designer. Preformed cascade and waterfall units are very inflexible compared with a liner, but they do have the advantage of being watertight if installed correctly. The greatest danger with a liner construction is not so much the risk of puncturing, but seepage around the edges if these are not very carefully finished.

When excavating a liner waterfall, commence work next to the pool and then progress up the incline. As with a mound for preformed units, it is equally important that the soil into which the liner is to be placed is compacted. This can be done artificially, but is much better achieved by full settlement following winter rain. Any sinking after the liner is installed may result in seepage.

With a lined construction there are often facings of rock and a covering of gravel or shingle. These can be arranged to produce wonderful effects, but always remember that it is the solid soil foundation and the protective layer of pool liner that enables attractive natural-looking features to be created and any deficiency will show later.

Using a pool liner and dressing the finished construction with rocks and gravels also enables different flow patterns to be created. A continual curtain of water results from a smooth uniform edge while violent tumbles can be arranged by forcing the water through narrow gaps in rocks and stones.

CONSTRUCTING A WATERFALL USING A LINER

1 *The soil is removed from a natural slope to create an excavation which is the finished size of the waterfall.*

2 *Line the excavation with underlay. This prevents stones or any other sharp objects from puncturing the liner.*

3 *Liner is spread out over the underlay. Ensure that there is sufficient overlap all around. Mold the liner to the trench.*

4 *Place the securing rocks firmly on the edge of the waterfall, creating as natural an appearance as possible.*

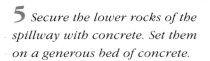
5 *Secure the lower rocks of the spillway with concrete. Set them on a generous bed of concrete.*

6 *At vulnerable points along the spillway, point the rocks with mortar to prevent seepage.*

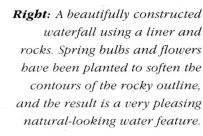

Right: *A beautifully constructed waterfall using a liner and rocks. Spring bulbs and flowers have been planted to soften the contours of the rocky outline, and the result is a very pleasing natural-looking water feature.*

7 *It is essential for a secure, consistent flow of water to cement the spillways at each part of the fall. Try to keep the stones level.*

8 *When all the rocks are securely in place any surplus pool liner should be cut off neatly. Edges can be disguised with topsoil.*

9 *Well-washed gravel is introduced to the waterfall pools. This disguises wrinkles in the liner and creates a useful wildlife habitat.*

a waterfall from preformed units

There are many and varied preformed waterfall and cascade units that can be added to a pool. Some look very natural, but others are hideous, so take time to select appropriate units carefully and be aware of how much will still be exposed once they are installed.

Some preformed units are single structures, while others comprise a series of separate sections of different configuration which offer imaginative design opportunities. None of the preformed units, whether reconstituted stone, plastic or fiberglass, are easy to install from the visual point of view. They really only look convincing when they are dressed with rocks and heavily planted. However, they are completely watertight and if installed correctly should become a leak-proof feature.

Preformed waterfall and cascade units have to be installed on a slope. This may be a natural feature or else created by soil profiling, but should be both tall and wide enough to accommodate their length and breadth without giving a cramped appearance. If an artificial mound has to be created, it should ideally be allowed to settle over the winter period. Installing preformed units on freshly disturbed soil results in slippage, and the whole construction process may have to be started again.

Preformed units can also be installed in a more formal manner where the land is terraced. They can be included very satisfactorily as an integral part of a formal water arrangement secured between stone or brick walls. The options for their imaginative use are legion.

To be really successful, their foundations must be firm and level. Unsettled soil, which causes twisting and seepage, can be a major problem. With new constructions, create a secure mound of hardcore and cover it with soil.

MAKING A WATERFALL FROM PREFORMED UNITS

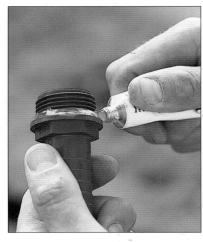

1 *To avoid the outlet hose from the pump showing above the water, drill a small hole through the back, ideally below the point at which the water level will rest in the upper part of the unit.*

2 *It is vital to seal the joint with the input hose with a waterproof sealant so that there is no prospect of water escaping. Any seepage behind the unit may result in soil slippage.*

3 *Allow the sealant to set properly after introducing the fitting. The outlet pipe is trimmed so that the fitting can be fixed securely with a plastic nut screwed flush to the unit.*

4 *An excavation larger than the cascade units is prepared to permit room for adjustment. The units are then placed in their final positions, bricks being used behind as necessary for packing.*

5 *The soil is then replaced carefully beneath and around the units. It is important that it fills all the voids.*

6 *When everything is finally in place and backfilled, it should be checked with a level. Also test the flow of water to see that it falls as you want it to.*

7 *The finished feature planted with water flowing freely – a simple method of introducing moving water into the garden.*

Above: *Preformed cascade units come in all shapes and sizes. Here an effective design of scalloped bowls lets water tumble down four levels.*

canals and rills

Canals and rills are a very artificial, but nonetheless attractive, means of moving water around the garden. They are quite intentionally formal, creating straight lines and angles rather than gracious curves or arcs.

A rill is generally regarded as being a very narrow shallow canal. It is a feature which can be used boldly to enhance and define the physical structure of a garden layout, or subtly to move water around. The gentle musical note created by the flow of the water, which moves like quicksilver in and around the plants, is often the only evidence of its presence.

Canals are different structures. In some cases they can be formally constructed ditches, moving large quantities of water from place to place, often with the intention of servicing a waterfall or water wheel. Occasionally they are adaptations created from natural water flows across a property. Where a stream flows naturally through a garden and the overall design is one of formality, then this can often be very successfully converted into a canal. Take care if making such an alteration not to interfere with the flow rate, as it might have an adverse effect upon neighboring properties both upstream and downstream.

More often than not, canals are created in order to divide or subdivide the garden in a formal way. They are often used to great effect where different levels are desired. Few plants enjoy life in a canal, and few settings

Left: *The formal use of water in small square ponds interconnected by rills divides the garden into convenient sections which can accommodate various plantings. The sound and movement of the flowing water and the use of fountain jets bring a hard landscape to life.*

Right: *This canal is wide enough to produce excellent reflections, yet at the same time is flowing quickly and producing a beautiful curtain of water. A high standard of maintenance is necessary in order to achieve this beautiful garden spectacle.*

would be enhanced by attempted plantings. A canal is essentially an unadorned, formal means for moving water. However, it can be constructed or dressed using a wide diversity of materials including colored tiles, slate or mosaic. The materials from which it is constructed should be the focus of attention visually, rather than any attempt at accompanying planting.

Above: *A rill need not be substantial to be effective. This attractive stone-faced channel in dappled shade creates all manner of highlights as the shallow water ripples across its stony bottom. The paving defines the edge and provides ready access for anyone wanting to walk near the water.*

making a canal or rill

A canal or channel is an exciting water garden feature, but one which really only fits into a formal garden design. It can be a feature for its own sake, or equally a means physically to separate parts of the garden. However it is contrived, it must have definite points to flow to and from. If creating a beginning and end point is not practical, then clever planting is necessary to ensure that it looks convincing.

A pond will often be the focal point, but it does not have to stand at the end of the feature as with a waterfall. A canal can equally pass through it, and by clever contrivance can be used to enable subtle level changes to take place with a small tumble of water.

A canal has to be very carefully blended into the garden design, especially with regard to the excavated soil. It may be simpler to dig out the canal and to place the soil on the banks, but this creates a very awkward and artificial appearance. A canal is generally better partially excavated and then the soil spread up to the construction; or, alternatively, constructed at soil level with the water source and any pool level predetermined, the ground being made up to the construction, rather than the canal sunk into the ground.

Canals can be constructed of a wide range of materials, but tile and wood are very serviceable and fashionable. Indeed, with the imaginative use of wood narrow rills and spouts can easily be constructed that carry water in attractively symmetrical aqueducts. Brick is also satisfactory. Concrete is often utilized, but is very functional in appearance and for most small canals should be used only as a last resort.

MAKING A TIMBER RILL

1 *Prepare the timber carefully, ensuring a neat tight fit. Bond the timber edges to the base using a strong adhesive. Clamp the lengths in position until the adhesive has set. Accuracy of construction at this stage is of great importance.*

2 *Once the main timber components have been secured by a waterproof adhesive, they should be screwed together. Drill pilot holes slightly smaller than the screws and then screw them in.*

3 *A small block of wood secures the end of the rill. This should be measured carefully and cut so that it can be successfully glued and then screwed in position to ensure a watertight seal.*

4 *The whole unit can now be painted liberally with a wood preservative. Choose one that will prevent the timber from rotting and that will dry completely so that there is never any pollution hazard to the water.*

5 *A hole is drilled in the end stop board of the rill so that a small hose can be fed in to deliver the water. This outlet can be disguised with plants as the final picture (right) reveals.*

Left: *A rill can take many forms, from a narrow stone gully to an elaborate metal chute like this which, by virtue of its elevation, creates an additional moving water element. It is a clean-cut, modern garden feature.*

streams and brooks

A stream or brook is the most natural form of flowing water. Gardeners who are lucky enough to have a natural feature like this which just requires dressing with plants or perhaps a slight adjustment of the flow are very lucky, especially if water flow is consistent for 12 months of the year.

This is the idyllic garden stream or brook, a lovely feature fed by a spring and which is not influenced or altered by rainfall. The other natural kind of stream depends upon rainfall or snowmelt and it may not always flow evenly. It can be subject to flooding as well as summer drought. This is a problematic scenario which is very difficult to incorporate successfully into a manicured garden.

The best stream or brook is one that does not depend upon the vagaries of nature and which is constructed by the gardener to fulfill the role that it needs to in the designated position in the garden. With careful calculations and construction, a most convincing stream can be created which will have constant clear water and not be adversely affected by natural phenomena.

Below: *An enchanting stream where water ripples over a gravelly bed and the flow is diverted by well-placed stones.*

Left: *Although this artificial stream bisects the garden, access across a discreet bridge enables it to be enjoyed from all sides.*

Below: *The best garden streams are usually created on a natural slope.*

A stream in the garden need not go to or come from anywhere in particular. It can emerge from a pile of rocks and disappear the same way, although it is more visually appealing if a stream is linked to a pond. This can either be situated above or below the stream feature – it really matters little. With the modern materials available, from flexible pool liners to preformed plastic stream units, artificial stream construction is among the easiest and most rewarding means of introducing moving water to a garden.

constructing a small stream

Streams are best constructed from a pool liner that is disguised completely by rocks, pebbles, stones and marginal planting. By using a liner it is possible to produce almost any shape or design that is desired. It is also easier to control and adjust the depth and fall of the stream so that the desired water flow is achieved.

The first considerations with a stream are the header outlet and the base pool, for it is difficult to produce a credible independent stream without having a pool at the base in which a submersible pump can be placed and a small header feature to which the water can be pumped. The length of the stream and the ability of the pump to move the water the distance and vertical height required also needs careful thought. It may be that by taking the stream around the garden while keeping its outlet quite close to the header, the pump delivery hose can be kept

MAKING A STREAM

1 *Mark out the outline of the stream bed with stakes or string before digging commences.*

2 *Dig the stream to the full depth taking into account the required slope to the pond.*

3 *Carefully expose the edge of the existing pool taking care not to puncture the liner.*

4 *Line with underlay, firming it down and ensuring that it molds to the stream's contours.*

5 *Lay the liner into the trench over the underlay and test that the water flow is satisfactory.*

6 *The pipe which carries the water to the head of the stream is laid in a narrow trench.*

7 *Once the liner has been installed, the stones that form the stream bed are laid in place.*

8 *Use large stones piled at the head of the stream to trap and conceal the outlet pipe.*

9 *The pool liner edge is tucked under the turf to create a neat and tidy finish.*

10 *Paddle stones are added to fill in any gaps between the larger slabs on the stream bed.*

11 *Lower the pump into the pool close to the stream. It will need to be quite powerful.*

much shorter than the overall length of the stream. This is important because the efficiency of the pump drops off the greater the height of the head of water required and the length of hose the water is pumped through.

The liner should ideally be all in one piece – rather than separate overlapping lengths – and it should be laid into a shallow excavation. It must also be spread well over the sides and tucked into the turf or concealed with edging material. If several pieces of liner do have to be used, ensure a generous overlap with the upper pieces overlapping the lower ones in the same manner as roof tiles. Once lined, the stream bed should be heavily dressed with slabs of stone and pebbles. Similarly large rocks and stones can be used to hide the sides of the stream, while occasionally provision can be made for a marginal plant to be established to assist in the disguise of the stream edges.

The flow of the stream can be greatly enhanced by the placement of attractive rocks in its course. These can be used to narrow the stream and squeeze the flow so that it tumbles faster, or placed in a position where the water dances over them and creates splashes and highlights.

Right: *An artificial stream is so much easier to manage than a natural one, yet with clever planting and the suitable placement of stones it can appear quite natural within its garden setting.*

ornamental fountains

Fountains are essentially jets of water in different configurations which are powered into the air and tumble back to the pond as sparkling droplets. Such simplicity is not always appreciated, however, and more elaborate means of dispensing the water is sought, often through the use of statuary.

In traditional gardens of European style statuary has made an important contribution to both design and ambiance. In its original form it was often constructed on a grand scale, especially where major water features were concerned, all manner of chariots and horses being apparently driven through a torrent of turbulent water. Such grandeur was only to be seen in the great gardens and squares of European cities, but these masterpieces set the pattern and provided the technical knowledge for a generation of impressively realistic and very functional classical ornamental fountains to be produced.

These varied from the water carrier and nymph to the comical frogs of the Peterhof in Russia and the small boy or *manneken pis*, a landmark in Brussels. Miniature water carriers, nymphs and comical frogs (as well as the Belgian boy) can all be purchased in excellent reproduction and merely need connecting to a submersible pump to become functional fountains. However, there are many other designs based upon characters in legend or birds and animals which are widely available from garden centers.

Left: This very modern water garden uses everything to brilliant and controversial excess. A larger-than-life waterlily produces pleasing water movement in a pond devoid of plants. Such uses of living plants or animals as designs upon which to base fountains and water features have a long tradition.

Right: The combinations of light and water movement and their importance when planning a moving water feature can be appreciated by looking at this beautifully sculptured fountain ornament. Of a traditional, classical design, it provides an important focal point in this symmetrical walled garden.

Some are made from stone, others concrete or reconstituted stone, while a few are of a hard plastic construction. These sometimes have to be partly filled with sand to give them stability.

Nowadays there is such a rich diversity of ornamental fountain pieces available that you can opt for the simplicity of a solitary water carrier or the tumbling, frothing fury of a Trevi-style fountain, or even aspire to a mixture of both.

Above: *The use of common materials in an unusual way can heighten the effect of moving water. Here the cunning deployment of a mirror greatly enhances the impression of water flowing over its surfaces.*

making a poolside feature

Moving water usually emanates from within the pond or else tumbles over a waterfall or cascade, but it is also perfectly possible to feature it at the side of the pond. The submersible pump is placed within the pond and the delivery hose carried to the top of the feature in much the same way as with a waterfall. It is important with such a feature to have a sufficiently powerful pump, since often there is a considerable distance and lift from pump to the water exit.

Poolside features are often formal and take the form of a raised tube or chute, or ornamental fountain heads. In such cases considerable quantities of water are moved, and the splash resulting from such water displacement is considerable. This should be considered very carefully from the beginning. Less formal arrangements – particularly units

or features that are manufactured for the purpose and where a gentle flow of water is preferred – are much easier to install.

At present there is a trend for creating leaves in fiberglass with connections and jets which enable them to be arranged rather like an artificial plant with water tumbling from leaf to leaf. The giant *Gunnera* or prickly rhubarb is a favorite from which to make impressions, although the leaves of ornamental rheum as well as the umbrella plant also known as *Darmera* are commonly available. On their own, even if arranged in natural array, they look rather stiff and fake, but once fully integrated with live vegetation they can be very pleasing, creating subtle sounds and movement of water.

MAKING A LEAF CASCADE

Left: *Even artificial leaves can look effective. They are a very practical way of bringing tumbling water into the garden.*

1 *Drill a hole in the leaf to accommodate the outflow pipe in the base of the Gunnera leaf. Use a hole saw drill fitting.*

2 *Insert a screw fitting and secure the outflow pipe from beneath with a clamp. To ensure that it attaches firmly, use a quick-setting bonding agent. It is important that the union between leaf and pipe is secure. Any seepage will reduce the flow rate.*

3 *Secure the outflow pipe to the pump outlet using a hose clamp. Ensure that only the waterfall outflow is functional and make any adjustments necessary to the control valve.*

Above: *This copper design makes very effective use of artificial plant leaves to create a softly flowing multi-tiered fountain.*

4 *It is possible to enhance the appearance of the leaf by using a spray paint aerosol. Use sparingly to create a subtle effect.*

5 *Having placed the first leaf, it is essential to test the water flow using a watering can to ensure that it pours out as desired.*

6 *The second leaf is placed in position. Then put the pump in the pond, conceal the pipework with plants and switch on.*

fountain spray patterns

The variety of spray patterns and shapes that can be achieved by using a modern submersible pump are legion. For the beginner a simple spray pattern is probably best to start with, greater elaboration coming with experience. Because spray patterns are created by removable attachments fitted to standard submersible pump units, the cost involved in making changes is very small. Indeed it is possible to accumulate a collection of fittings that will provide a range of spray patterns that can be changed according to personal whim.

Traditionally there have been rules which relate to successful fountain usage, although these are interpreted according to individual circumstances. In windy gardens it is wise to restrict the height of any jet or spray pattern to half the radius of the pool. Where conditions are calmer in a more sheltered garden, the jet of water can be equal in height to the diameter of the pond or basin.

Simple single fountain jets are often used as a focal point, but they can also serve to divide a space or interrupt a vista, encouraging the visitor to pause before moving on. Single-jet fountains are also used in asymmetric designs to offset and balance another nearby garden feature. With multiple spray patterned jets, there are no particular guidelines to consider. Just attach the fountain jet and enjoy.

When selecting an appropriate spray arrangement, do not overlook the possibilities of combining it with lighting. Few garden features can compare with moving water which is lit at night.

A simple divided jet which produces large droplets of water. These are best used in positions where light can play on the water.

A bell fountain offers the calmest use of moving water. It is often used in peaceful corners where there are no other distractions.

The standard sprinkle fountain jet for the small pool. It produces a pleasing visual effect and at the same time creates magical sounds.

Right: *Water geysers can be created in the home garden by the use of a strong jet which mixes air and water and is attached to a powerful submersible pump.*

installing a pond fountain

The installation of a fountain in a pond is relatively simple if a modern submersible pump is utilized. Considerable output can be achieved by a small pump which is discreet and easy to hide. Sometimes a pump may be situated conveniently immediately beneath a fountain ornament, rocks or other decorative feature. This is generally the most satisfactory arrangement as the water is then delivered for the shortest distance.

It is possible to install a pump which takes water to a remote spray head, but full account must be taken of the distance the water has to travel and the strength of pump necessary both to move the water and to produce the desired spray effect. In such circumstances it is necessary to disguise the pump. This method of concealment should be as simple and uncluttered as possible to permit access and maintenance when necessary. By creating a raised rocky outcrop

beneath which the pump can be hidden, a suitable resting or hiding place is coincidentally made available for the fish.

Whatever arrangement is decided upon, for successful fountain installation it is essential that the pump is both level and accessible. It should be possible regularly and easily to remove and clean the input filter as debris getting into the water flow and blocking the fountain jet is one of the greatest irritations for the pond owner and a constant detraction from the fountain's beauty. The electrical cable must also be dealt with safely and carefully, wherever possible its exit point from the pool being situated beneath a carefully placed rock at the water's edge.

Right: Not one, but two fountains are used to produce this interesting effect. Both will require separate installation and individual pumps, but they may occupy the same plinth.

ADDING A FOUNTAIN TO A POND

1 *When preparing a plinth for a fountain, it is important to work out the scale of the construction and to calculate the height at which the pump must be situated to create the desired effect. To protect the pool liner, protective liner underlay should be laid before construction of the plinth begins.*

2 *A paving slab having being laid and leveled as the foundation, work can begin. Ordinary house bricks are laid using a standard mortar. For a plinth up to three bricks high, you may lay the bricks directly upon one another. Larger ones require staggered brickwork.*

3 *The top of the plinth is made from a paving slab. It is very important that this is absolutely level from side to side and end to end in order that the pump sits evenly and securely.*

4 *The pump should be level on the plinth. The plinth can also support a fountain ornament with the pump hidden beneath.*

5 *You can use a hook secured to a stick to lower the pump onto the plinth if you do not want to wade into the water to do this.*

6 *With the pump installed, it is simply a matter of plugging it into the electricity supply and switching on. Providing that the jet is positioned just clear of the water surface, the fountain will swing into full and effective action immediately.*

wall fountains and grottoes

It is possible to enjoy moving water without a pond, but in a confined space it can be difficult to achieve this effectively. Wall fountains and grottoes provide the imaginative gardener with a viable option, both for home construction and for building in kit form. Indeed, some wall fountains are completely self-contained and merely require hanging on the wall, filling with water and connecting to an electrical supply.

There are a number of masks and gargoyles that can be used to spout water into a container below. This may be a small pool or just a modest bowl or dish. In some cases the water may not be circulated directly from this, but rather from a reservoir or sump hidden behind or beneath the display. In this way the only visible feature is the gargoyle or wall mask from which a stream of water gently spouts.

Grottoes are wonderful adjuncts to a garden. They conjure up a mystical or contemplative atmosphere and can become important focal points in the garden. Simplicity is the keynote for a grotto's success. Plain moss-covered stones and gentle dripping water conjure up the image of legends, while in the family suburban garden a grotto can become the haunt of friendly garden gnomes and fairies, much to the delight of small children.

Of all the moving water features, wall fountains and grottoes probably offer the greatest freedom of expression since they can be whatever you want them to be: traditional, modern, mystical or abstract. With these features the unconventional gardener can get away with almost anything!

Above: *An interesting concept is this fountain in reverse. Inside the grotto the water is directed downwards from the ceiling into a pool below.*

Right: *The art of moving water in the classical style. This grotto embraces all traditions from clam shells and a mask of Apollo to tufa rock.*

ram's head wall fountain

Wall fountains have a great tradition, and modern versions of the masks and gargoyles of the past are widely available from garden centers. They provide a very versatile method of introducing moving water into the smaller garden without diminishing its importance. Apart from masks and gargoyles, there are also many types of wall fountains which are completely self-contained and flow into a raised or sunken basal pool, a bowl or dish.

Wall masks and gargoyles are available in all sorts of styles and in materials ranging from reconstituted stone and lead to terracotta, fiberglass and plastic. Their appearance is obviously important, but so is that of the container into which the water is to spout. This must be of a size and capacity which will accommodate the spray, but also be of a pleasing appearance and in visual conformity with its surroundings.

Consideration must also be given to the wall to which the fountain is attached. Old solid walls create difficulty with disguising the discharge pipe from the pump, and chasing a groove into the wall is often the only option. Unless carefully undertaken, this can look ugly. The ideal is to attach the fountain to a cavity wall and take the pipe up through the cavity where it will be out of sight. When all else fails, use an attractive pipe as a virtue.

HANGING A WALL FOUNTAIN

1 *Masks and gargoyles are not the easiest features to fit successfully. It is best to make all the connections in mock-up first before drilling the holes in the wall and committing to its fixing. Make sure that all the connections and the screw holes in the mask function before fitting begins.*

2 *Mark the positions precisely, holding the mask in position against the wall. Once the drilling points have been established, go ahead and drill the holes and insert suitable plugs. They expand as the screws are inserted and hold the mask to the wall.*

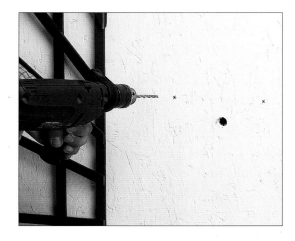

3 *Secure the mask firmly in place making certain that all the pipe work and connections on the other side of the wall are in the correct position.*

PLANTING SUGGESTIONS

Plants Used
Canna glauca hybrid/summer/marginal
Cyperus eragrostis/summer/marginal
Iris laevigata 'Variegata'/summer/marginal

Alternative Plants
Ranunculus lingua 'Grandiflorus'/
    summer/marginal
Schoenoplectus tabernaemontani
    'Zebrinus'/summer/marginal

4 *There are usually covers or caps provided to disguise the screw heads and to conceal the method of fastening. Fit these and make sure that they are secure, sealing as necessary. The fountain is then ready for connection and use.*

5 *Connect the pump to the outlet and place it in position in the reservoir pool, disguising the outflow pipe at the same time. It is prudent to check water output at this time.*

6 *Add suitable plants. Take account of the water level and only introduce those that are compatible; one should not dominate the others. Select only those plants that do not object to constantly splashing water.*

Right: *An attractive arrangement for a small garden with plenty of opportunities for enjoying plants, fish and the magic of moving water.*

adding decorative touches

While a traditional water garden containing pleasingly arranged plants and colorful fish is the goal of most water gardeners, this is not the whole story. There are many other additions that can be made which will greatly enhance a feature. Some of these are of standard manufacture, while others can be constructed by the imaginative gardener.

The most important addition to a pond, apart from moving water, is garden lighting. There are underwater lights, both those that can be tucked among marginal plants as well as special up-lighters for fountains, and surface lights that can be positioned around a pool.

Pond edges can be decorative too. Attractive paving in varied arrangements as well as timber, planted coir rolls or decking all add to the visual attraction of a pool. Streams and rills can be crossed by bridges and causeways. Even if they are not required for serious foot traffic, such bridges can be positioned to great decorative effect, and at the same time they offer an opportunity for viewing the water garden from a different angle.

In the larger feature an island can be included. Simple static islands present a range of opportunities for the introduction of interesting plants, while floating islands are much sought after as a safe haven for wildlife.

Ornaments of various kinds have long been used for adding a little extra flourish to a water garden. From the traditional classical statue that stands spouting water at the poolside, to minimalist constructions, mirrors and fountain arrangements which employ glass, steel or timber in modern configurations, there is a world of choice.

*An **ammonite** provides the focal point of this gentle stream.*

decking

Decking is an extremely popular landscape material. Most decking is of high-quality timber, but there are synthetic and often recycled materials also available. Originally timber decking was offered as a rustic means of achieving various objectives with walkways, causeways and sitting-out areas, but now it has become fashionable to paint it in all manner of interesting 'designer' shades.

From the point of view of the water gardener, when decking is suitable visually, it can provide the most

Right: *The extensive use of decking here not only provides a neat edge to the poolside – it has become an important part of the water feature in its own right. The timber harmonizes with the water, and offers an area for poolside recreation without detracting from the importance of the pool itself.*

Left: *A combination of natural materials – the informality of the stones and gravel contrasts with the formality of the beautifully shaped decking. Timber is a very versatile edging material, conveniently disguising what lies beneath.*

Lower right: *Apart from providing a neat solution to edging a water feature, decking can also provide access, as here by means of a causeway. If carefully planned, the structure can contribute positively to the ambiance of the water feature.*

useful and functional of pond edging. Not only is it a first-class disguise to conceal the ugly edge of a pond, but, when properly and sturdily constructed, it is an ideal place from which to survey and enjoy one's watery endeavors.

Decking can also be used to great effect as a causeway across a large expanse of water, or as a landing stage or a similar extension into the pool, allowing the water to be appreciated from a different viewpoint.

Although rarely treated as a background for plantings, when handled in this manner decking can be extremely

effective, especially for surrounding and isolating individual plant specimens. This applies both in the water with taller marginal subjects as well as on drier land where soil conditions are more regular and stately architectural plants, like bamboos and rheums, flourish. Such plants are wonderful for the backdrop of a water garden and their foliage can soften the angular harshness of some traditional decking and assist in uniting the water feature with the rest of the garden.

making your own decking

As decking has become increasingly popular, it is now quite easy to purchase timber suitable for decking projects from local timber suppliers or garden centers. While decking used to employ standard timber treated with a wood preservative, nowadays it is available in an array of specially manufactured configurations, usually weatherproofed. The deckboards are made with longitudinally grooved surfaces which are not only non-slip, but also visually appealing.

When it comes to making your own decking, the first and most important consideration is to purchase the best quality timber that you can afford. Cheap timber sparingly treated with preservative not only looks poor, but will have a very limited life.

It is vital to ensure that all supports for decking are substantial; timber uprights should be at least 4 in. (10 cm) square and either set in concrete or dropped into a metal fencing sleeve or pipes set into concrete. The maximum distance between structural posts should be 6 ft. (180 cm.). The boards themselves are mostly 6 in. (15 cm.) wide, although it is possible to get both narrower and wider deckboards. The gap between boards when they are fastened to the subframe should be no more than 0.2 in. (5 mm.); make sure that whatever gap you leave is consistent across the whole deck. The space permits the timber to move in different weather conditions and lets rainwater drain away freely. Remember to treat any sawn ends with a proprietary sealer to make them weatherproof.

Decking screws are now widely available and are the best method of securing the timbers to their supports, although there is still a place for bolts, especially where strong uprights require connecting. Alternatively, galvanized deck ties can be used to secure boards to the joists. The successful construction of decking depends upon careful planning and accurate measurements. But with some forward planning, it is not as complex a task as it may at first appear.

CONSTRUCTING A DECKING PLATFORM

1 *The timber framework for decking should be substantial and the individual bearers placed at intervals to provide good support. These should be set no more than 18 in. (45 cm) apart, but ideally 12 in. (30 cm), especially over water.*

2 *Having ensured that the framework is square and tightly secured, the first deckboard is placed in position at the desired angle. Start at one corner of the framework and work outwards.*

3 *Secure the first board using decking screws. These are best screwed in using a power screwdriver. Prior to fastening it down, square off each end of this board so that it will lie flush with the frame.*

4 Position the boards so that a straight edge can be placed on them and the angle at which each has to be cut can be marked with a pencil line. Ensure a small gap between each for subsequent fixing.

Left: Well-constructed decking provides an ideal edge for a formal pool. Not only is it neat and pleasing to the eye, but it provides safe and easy access to the waterside for both pond maintenance and enjoyment. When installing decking, it is important to provide strong supports and to ensure that it is level in all directions. Only use purpose-made deckboards and ensure that they have been pressure-treated with a wood preservative that is harmless to fish and plant life.

5 The gap between boards to allow for timber movement and surface drainage need only be minimal, but it should be uniform. The end of a carpenter's pencil can be utilized as a convenient unit of measure.

6 The boards are placed in position and secured with decking screws, at least two being used at each support point. It is important to ensure that they screw vertically into the timber for a secure fit.

7 There is usually a small carpentry task required at the end to ensure a neat finish. It is possible to run the decking out to an even number of boards, but this rarely produces ideal overall dimensions.

using ready-made decking

In the past decking was often overwhelmingly linear in appearance. All the boards ran in the same direction, the only concessions being made at the corners where for strength, convenience and appearance right-angled joints were usually created.

With the increasing and widespread use of decking, manufacturers and designers have appreciated that it need not be simply functional, but can be an integral part of the designed landscape, making a major visual contribution to the outside living space. However, using just straight lengths of timber, the home gardener would have to be a reasonably skilled carpenter to achieve interesting patterns and variations that will have a powerful visual impact.

Realizing the limitations of the average home do-it-yourselfer, manufacturers have now come up with ready-made decking shapes in a series of appealing patterns and configurations. Squares of decking are the most popular, but hexagons, octagons, circles and other shapes are now freely available, many of which can be mixed and matched with one another. Elaborate features can be easily realized with modern decking squares.

While these can be used as part of traditional decking construction, they are also versatile enough to be attractively arranged to create landing stages and piers, the fixing arrangements being identical to those used for conventional decking construction, but with additional supports when several shapes are utilized together.

Left: *Ready-made decking can be used to create wonderful design effects as well as to fulfill a function in the garden. It is very important when decking extends over the water that it has adequate support, especially when it is to be routinely used for recreational purposes, such as standing or sitting. Looking good is not enough; the structure must be safe as well.*

USING DECKING SQUARES

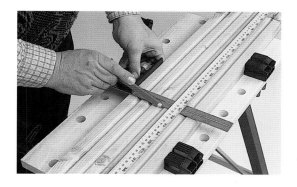

1 *Measure and cut the support timbers so that they correspond exactly with the dimensions of the decking square.*

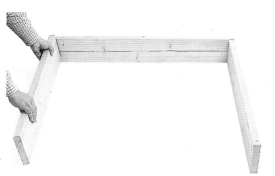

2 *Once cut to length, position the timbers in a square and check that the decking top fits exactly. Then screw the base together.*

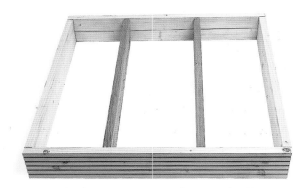

3 *Provide central bearers to ensure that the platform is fully supported. Once the legs are secured, these will be screwed into position.*

4 *Using decking screws and a power screwdriver, fasten the boards that form the edge of the platform to the support legs.*

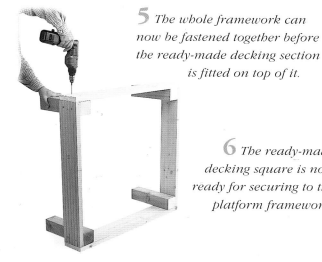

5 *The whole framework can now be fastened together before the ready-made decking section is fitted on top of it.*

6 *The ready-made decking square is now ready for securing to the platform framework.*

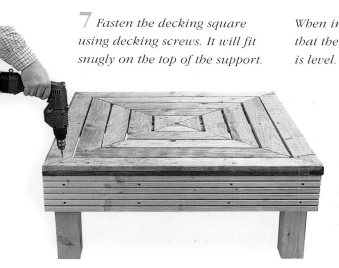

7 *Fasten the decking square using decking screws. It will fit snugly on the top of the support.*

When installed, ensure that the platform is level.

lighting

It seems improbable that electrical lighting should be associated with water, but in fact it can be a harmonious partner. Not only does it highlight plants or objects located on the bank, but it can also be used within the pond as well. Modern garden lights of suitable manufacture can be placed almost anywhere within or around the pond – submerged lights being particularly effective.

Of course electricity and water can be dangerous bedfellows, but modern wiring circuits using transformers and low-voltage cables ensure that there is no danger of personal electrocution, nor of decimating the fish population. Providing that all the manufacturer's instructions are followed, there is no reason why pond and garden lighting cannot become a permanent, safe and most enjoyable feature of the garden landscape.

While most garden lighting draws on the electricity from the house or garage, increasingly solar energy is coming to the fore as a power source. How well this performs depends largely upon where you live and how much sunlight your garden receives, although some manufacturers have developed a system whereby recharging takes place even in cloudy conditions so lights can operate almost whatever the weather.

Below: Underwater and external lighting can transform a pond in the evening, creating a magical effect with shadows and reflections.

However, for the best and most reliable light, electricity is to be preferred. It is bright and consistent. Apart from highlighting static features, it can be used to uplight fountain sprays, not only with white light, but also with an array of contrasting colors when used with tinted lenses. These need not be static colors, for it is possible to attach a rotating disk containing several different lenses beneath a fountain jet to produce a rainbow of delight.

Left: Lighting can be used to highlight the rushing and tumbling of water. When combined with a fogger unit, turbulent rapids become an atmospheric river of fire.

Above: The most spectacular use of lighting is with a decorative fountain feature. Carefully placed uplighting can bring a touch of grandeur to a small water garden.

installing in-pool lighting

It is vital when installing lighting to have a very healthy respect for electricity, especially when it is in close proximity to water. Potentially this is a deadly combination. However, there should be no problem with in-pond lights providing that a reputable brand is purchased and all the instructions that are given with the equipment are adhered to properly.

Underwater lighting is quite safe – modern units are manufactured to operate with low-voltage cable and a transformer, and the light units themselves are specially sealed. For the best effect, underwater lighting can be placed beneath a fountain or waterfall feature to illuminate the tumbling water. Alternatively it can be situated at the edge of the pool pointing inwards to focus upon a particular ornament or plant grouping, or outwards to illuminate an object on the pond edge. The placement of lights is not an exact science and it may be necessary to reposition the lights several times before the desired effect is achieved.

This is where floating lights can come into their own. These function in exactly the same manner as static underwater lights but are more readily adjusted to suit prevailing conditions. Along with other electrical systems, it pays to think about what effects you want to create early in the planning stages of pond construction, so that not only can lighting positions be selected, but the necessary electrical connection points can be established close at hand. Floating candles are another 'low-tech' way of lighting a pond, but of course they are vulnerable to the prevailing weather conditions and likely to blow out on a windy night.

Some fountains have integral lights, which do not require any particular installation skills. However, it is important to position the fountain feature and pump on a secure flat plinth, and ideally in a position where the cable can be discreetly hidden as it enters the pond.

Above: *In-pool lighting can be most effective when used to highlight specific plants or pond ornaments. It is safe to use and available in a wide range of packages. Most have a transformer and white lights (right). However, the color can be changed by clipping on a different lens. Some pond lighting kits have a mechanism for attaching them to a pump – this can rotate to give several timed color changes.*

ATTACHING LIGHTS TO A FOUNTAIN

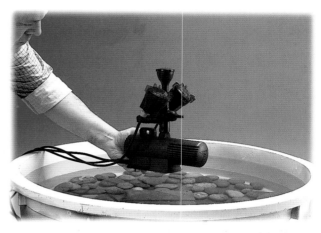

1 One of the most effective lighting arrangements simply clips the spotlight to a pump beneath the fountain head.

2 The color of the light can be changed by the use of differently colored lenses which snap on to make a watertight seal.

3 The submersible pump and lights are placed into position in the pool. The lights point upwards beneath the fountain.

4 When switched on, the light should illuminate all the spray pattern. Slight adjustment of the lights may be necessary.

Right: An underwater spotlight need not be attached to a pump. Free-standing lights can also produce dramatic effects.

installing external lights

The majority of exterior garden lights are installed after construction of the water feature is complete. Indeed it is often not until the pond is up and working that lighting is considered. It can then be tricky to achieve exactly the desired effect. It is better to regard lighting as an integral part of the project from the outset so that any underground cables or weatherproof power sockets can be carefully incorporated into the original plan.

Water and electricity are not compatible in most situations, so it is important to use only purpose-designed outdoor lighting and to follow installation instructions to the letter. The majority of outdoor garden lighting systems operate from a transformer that is linked to the household power source. The transformer reduces the voltage to a safe level, which means that the low-voltage cables from the transformer to the light units can be run quite safely along the surface of the ground, or concealed among the surrounding plants.

This is particularly useful as it allows major adjustments to be made after the lights have been positioned and permits a certain amount of experimentation with the uplighting of various garden features and plants. No underground wiring is required unless the transformer is installed in a building away from the house. The lamps can be fitted anywhere along the cable by means of a simple screw connection and are completely portable.

Once the positioning of the lights has been determined, it may be considered desirable to bury the cable so that it does not catch on a hoe or fork while you are undertaking routine tasks. In this case use conduit to thread it through and install in a similar way to the method illustrated, which is recommended for armored cables.

MAKING IT SAFE

It is important with external lighting that every precaution is taken to guarantee safety. Waterproof connectors and plugs are essential, as is a system which uses a transformer to eliminate the risk of accidents. Follow the maker's instructions carefully.

SETTING UP EXTERNAL LIGHTS

1 *The modern garden lighting kit is safe and reliable. However, follow instructions at all times – don't be tempted to improvise.*

2 *A transformer ensures that the electrical power output into the garden is stepped down to a safe voltage.*

3 *When fixing the lights, determine the position you want them to be and then screw the connectors into the cable.*

4 *Any external cable carrying mains power should be of a waterproof armored kind and laid in a conduit inside a trench.*

5 *Plastic cable conduits have snap-on covers that keep the wire safe from any disturbance by spade or fork.*

6 *Once the conduit is securely positioned in the foot of the trench, cover it over with a generous layer of builder's sand.*

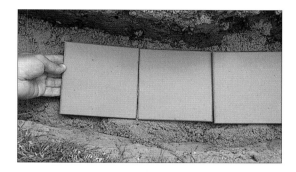

7 *Cover the cable with tiles for additional protection. This is a sensible precaution to protect it from future disturbance.*

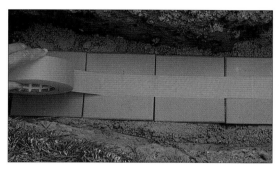

8 *Stretch electrical hazard tape along the run of tiles. This gives immediate warning of danger in case it should be unearthed*

9 *The individual lights are positioned discreetly at the poolside and focused upon carefully selected features in the pond.*

Above and right: *An entire water feature can be lit to give a dramatic appearance at night. Alternatively waterfalls, fountains or bridges can be selectively highlighted.*

stepping stones

The best way to cross a shallow band of water is by walking on stepping stones. Not only are they visually appealing and easily installed, but they are great fun, especially for children. It almost seems as if you are walking on water.

Stepping stones can also be used to divert the flow of water in a stream. Their presence can narrow the channel or push the water in varying directions, effectively increasing or decreasing the flow. Apart from the visual effect that this may have, the turbulence created also changes the sound of moving water.

Stepping stones were originally natural stones that were placed in the water at strategic points to enable passage from one bank to another. Any flat-topped stones were used. This is still the most attractive and natural method of creating a crossing, although from a safety point of view each stone should have a level upper surface and be able to generously accommodate a large foot.

Choosing natural stones carefully is important – many of those derived from sandstone or limestone are so soft that they shale and disintegrate when exposed to very cold temperatures in water. The surface should also have a grip so that there is no danger of slipping; some of the granites and millstone grits are excellent in this respect.

Nowadays garden centers are full of different kinds of manufactured stepping stones made from both concrete and reconstituted stone. They are all excellent; the only decision to make is the choice of the shape, texture or color that suits you best.

Below: *Stepping stones enable the garden visitor to traverse the water and also to view the pond from a different perspective. Although functional, stepping stones should also ideally be decorative.*

Above: *Stepping stones and paving can be used in a variety of configurations and associations with a water garden. They provide a means of crossing the water, but they also compartmentalize it and so become an integral part of the design. The use of the urn as a highlight to lift the eye, together with the careful positioning of plants with varying leaf forms, adds much to this arrangement.*

Left: *The placement of stepping stones need not be conventional. Their arrangement in diamond shapes and multiple groups makes a refreshing change and provides an excellent complement to the adjacent parterre hedging.*

laying stepping stones

The installation of stepping stones requires some care. The positions selected should first of all be visually appealing. Stepping stones can be an intrusion rather than an asset in a water feature when poorly placed. Of course they must also be functional and easy to traverse, at the same time being secure and level.

Stepping stones are almost inevitably placed after construction has been completed and water added to the feature. In the case of a natural watercourse, it is difficult to assess their ideal position accurately with regard to depth unless water is flowing freely and at an average depth. However, this can create difficulties with installation, as stepping stones are ideally placed when the water is at its lowest level. The perfect solution with a naturally variable water course is to take average water depth measurements and then position the stepping stones at a time of minimal flow.

In an artificial situation this is not a problem. Water levels are either known, or if uncertain are tested, and then the stepping stones installed appropriately. The relationship of the surface of the stones to the level of the water can be easily assessed.

Whether the installation of stepping stones is in an artificial stream or pond, or for traversing a natural flow of water, stability is essential. The stones must be securely concreted or affixed to a level base and positioned sufficiently close to one another so that anyone crossing can do so with a normal gait. Take care to choose stones that have a naturally roughened surface – smooth surfaces are likely to become slippery when wet.

Below: *Stepping stones are often principally for decoration. When used functionally, they must be placed at convenient even distances apart, ideally slightly closer than the length of an average stride.*

LAYING STONES ON PLINTHS

1 *A generous mortar bed must be laid to enable a level brick base for each stepping stone to be constructed.*

2 *Start by positioning bricks in the corners. Ensure that these are set square. This base should be smaller than the stepping stone.*

3 *Continue to lay bricks, ensuring that each is laid on an even mortar bed and is separated from the next by a layer of mortar.*

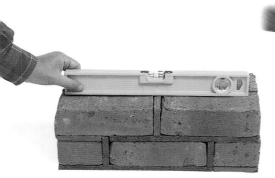

4 *Continue construction with the joints of the bricks arranged in an alternate fashion. Check regularly to ensure that they are level.*

5 *A final layer of mortar is applied when the desired height has been reached in order to secure the stepping stone.*

6 *Place the stepping stone gently into position on the mortar bed and firm into place. There should be a slight overhang.*

7 *Tap the stepping stone gently into position and make sure that it is level. Remove surplus mortar.*

A stepping stone is rather like an iceberg, the majority of the structure being beneath the water. A strong construction of this kind is absolutely essential to ensure personal safety.

bridges and causeways

Where there is a stream, rill or other ribbon of water in a garden, there is a natural desire to bridge it so that it can be viewed from another angle. There is also something entrancing about standing above water and viewing it from an overhead perspective. Bridges have long been the means of doing this, although across more open stretches of water or boggy ground raised causeways may be used.

Some bridges are very simple and it is their lack of an elaborate structure which gives them their charm. A plain length of stone or a single plank of timber can be functional in enabling you to cross a tiny rill or stream, but it also adds visual appeal to the garden scene. Likewise the traditional clapper bridge with its minimal support enchants the eye by its simplicity.

Bridges in a garden rarely exist solely as a functional means to cross water. Indeed, in some cases water is an excuse to build a bridge which is intended to become an

Below: A highly decorative bridge is the focal point of this garden. The glassy stillness of the water allows for pleasing reflections.

Above: A causeway permits the enjoyment of waterlilies and other aquatic plants at close quarters. In addition, it provides easy access for maintenance and contributes positively to the overall aquascape.

important focal point or garden feature. Some specially manufactured bridges are as intricate, expensive and elaborate as the most desirable pergola or summer house. These are often manufactured like furniture and sold in flat-packs for on-site assembly. More elaborate and expensive creations tend to come ready-made to place in position and they are best installed by a contractor.

Of course bridges do not have to be prefabricated. Although the majority of those seen in the home garden will be of such manufacture, DIY construction from stone or brick is a further option, but not one for the novice or faint-hearted handyman.

making a wooden bridge

A wooden bridge or causeway provides an opportunity to see the water garden from another angle. Although they should be visually appealing, most wooden bridges are first and foremost functional. They are used rather than viewed.

Any bridge or causeway construction must have a secure foundation. This is not only necessary for the safe passage of people, but also ensures stability. Even a modest bridge can settle under its own weight if it is built with insufficient foundations. Ideally the bridge should be attached by bolts to concrete piers sunk into the ground to a depth of about 2 ft. (60 cm). These are best cast in place and the bolts positioned in the concrete while it is still wet.

A causeway is really an extended bridge which takes the visitor across a large body of water, or alternatively criss-crosses a small water feature in an indirect fashion. Unlike a bridge where piers are created on either bank, a causeway is also attached to piers in the water.

The simplest method of creating supports for a causeway is to set short lengths of pipe into a concrete slab, or to bolt metal post supports to sturdy breeze blocks. The wooden supports for the bearers that will carry the planks of the causeway are dropped into these pipes after positioning in the pond. When such piers are created in a lined pool, it is important that they rest on a generous layer of fleece underlay to prevent damage to the liner.

In the creation of a wooden bridge or causeway, consider in which direction the timber planks lie. It is an established fact that if timbers are lying lengthways leading away from the bank, you are inclined to cross; if fastened crossways, you will probably linger on the bridge.

MAKING A WOODEN CAUSEWAY

1 *It is essential to have bolts firmly secured into the concrete basal supports.*

2 *Bolt the metal sleeves that will hold the bridge supports securely to the base.*

3 *Put the timber supports into the metal sleeves and make sure they are vertical.*

4 *Clamp a cross-member to each upright making sure that it is level. Use this as a template for the positioning of the other supports.*

Left: *The completed causeway – a neat and very economical method of bridging water attractively.*

5 *Secure each cross-piece with bolts in predrilled countersunk holes. It is imperative that all cross-members and supports align.*

6 *Drill the lengths of timber that are to form the walkway and secure them to the supports using substantial bolts.*

7 *Where there is a change in alignment of the causeway, make provision for the boards to fit neatly and evenly together.*

Above: *A causeway constructed from timber is an asset for both informal and formal water features. An offset arrangement of walkways like this breaks up the regularity of the construction, and encourages the walker to linger and admire the pool.*

installing an arched bridge

It is quite feasible to build an arched bridge from scratch, but it is more usual to purchase such a feature either ready-made or as a kit for self-assembly. When purchasing a kit or finished bridge, take care to ensure that all the dimensions are appropriate from both the practical and visual point of view. Also look carefully at the intended site before purchasing the bridge.

Even modest bridges are a considerable weight and must have sound foundations from both the point of view of safety and gradual settlement. If the soil slips, the bridge can twist and be damaged. So it is imperative that the positions of both ends of the bridge are thoroughly inspected and that suitable piers can be constructed to take the weight.

To be safe, the footings for each pier should be excavated to a depth of 2 ft. (60 cm). Bridge piers can be precast, but it can be simpler in most cases to cast them in position. For most bridges, digging holes of sufficient dimensions and filling them with concrete is adequate. Take care on clay soils which shrink badly and, where appropriate, include reinforcing rods in the piers.

When precast piers are used then dig the holes at least 6 in. (15 cm) larger all around than the piers themselves. Place them in position and pour in concrete. Alternatively you can build brick piers in the manner illustrated. Check that the piers on either bank are level and then install the bridge.

Right: *An arched bridge is an attractive focal point in many water gardens. The subtle curving form echoes the sinuous flow of water past the planted margins.*

SETTING UP A READY-MADE BRIDGE

1 *Create a level base for pier construction using mortar.*

2 *Lay bricks in an alternate arrangement to create piers.*

3 *Decide where the uprights will fit and mark the section of board that will have to be removed.*

4 *Cut out the slots that will accommodate the uprights for the curved handrail.*

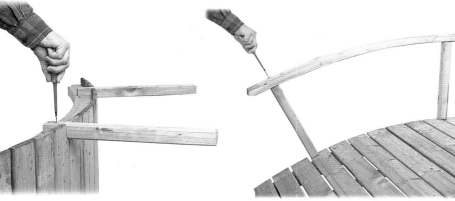

6 *Fasten the handrail securely. Ensure that the screws are countersunk for safety.*

7 *Drill holes through the base of the bridge to accommodate long screws. Change to a masonry drill bit when the drill reaches the bricks.*

5 *Screw the components together using rust-proof decking screws. The uprights should be evenly spaced along the bridge.*

8 *Long masonry fixings are inserted into the holes. Then the bridge is screwed securely to the brick piers.*

Above: *There are a variety of wood paints for garden features that can be used to decorate small bridges like this.*

islands

Islands generally look out of place in a small pond, since they also have to be small. Thus they lose much of their meaning and *raison d'être*. In addition a small island is much more difficult to construct than one of reasonable dimensions. Occasionally preformed pools offer an apology for an island in their design. Rarely are these of any great beauty, even when appropriately planted.

Even when an island is visually appropriate to a pond, its function is often not primarily a decorative one, but rather it is intended to provide a predator-free sanctuary for

Right: Islands look best visually when surrounded by sufficient water. In most water gardens, a well-planted island such as this looks completely natural, but in reality it is contrived. Where a tree or shrubs can be included, this is a great advantage, especially for the dull winter months. Here an Oriental feel is conveyed by the beautifully shaped pine tree, although the peripheral plantings are in the western tradition.

Left: When it comes to a formal pool, an artificial island is much more in keeping. Square or circular islands which reflect the shape of the pond are most pleasing to the eye. These can also be used for some highly colored planting – especially when built as dry islands, where bedding plants can be used.

wildlife. Such an island can usually be satisfactorily accommodated in a pond with minimum dimensions of 15 x 15 ft. (4.5 x 4.5 m).

The construction of islands, although wide and varied in method and material, is best carried out after the pond has been created. Unless the pond is to be a natural earth-bottomed structure sealed with bentonite clay, then much better control over the island structure can be achieved if it is added afterwards.

In a pond erosion of the island's margins is a potential problem and construction has to take this into account, while at the same time striving for as natural an appearance as possible. Few islands are appealing unless

Below right: *A contrast in styles – the peacefulness of the grass islands set off by their silver surrounds and the glassy stillness of the water is challenged by the riotous red planting in the borders and urns behind. These are built as dry islands isolated from the pond.*

planted, so suitable provision must be made for successful establishment of a variety of plants. Although an island is surrounded by water, it is possible to isolate it from this influence by the use of liner or brick walls in order to create dry conditions on the island itself. So, while the planting of 'wet' islands in most cases will consist of appropriately marginal or bog garden plants, if the soil within is separated from the water by a liner, summer bedding may be more appropriate in a 'dry' island.

making a wet island

One of the easiest and most effective islands to create is one built of sandbags. Such is the versatility of these malleable shapes that it is possible to achieve quite sophisticated arrangements by grouping them together, as well as ones of formal design. Sandbags are readily available from builders' suppliers and can be filled with either sand or soil as desired.

Using sand has the advantage of greater malleability and, although it is significantly heavier than soil, it does not contain nutrients which might escape into the water and create an algae problem. On the other hand the island is never going to become a real one from the plants' point of view, since roots are not going to penetrate the sand significantly and bind the island together. Indeed, a few years down the road, if not properly maintained with a consistent level of water, the burlap may rot, the sand spill out and the island disintegrate.

Soil in the bags will be bound together by roots and become a solid island, but there are considerable hazards of the nutrients in the soil leaching out into the surrounding water. Even if the lower bags are filled with sub-soil or clay, which is relatively inert, those in the upper layers where the plants are growing will be vulnerable to nutrient escape. However, algae and slimes will rapidly colonize the burlap and it will come to look quite natural.

The plants which will be established on sandbag islands will be bog or marginal subjects. A sandbag island is a wet island, the water table being at the level of the water in the pond which surrounds it, and so marginal and bog plants will thrive in this damp habitat.

MAKING A SANDBAG ISLAND

1 *Fill sandbags with river sand. Ensure that they are all of consistent size and shape.*

2 *Arrange the sandbags rather like bricks in alternate fashion to form a solid construction.*

3 *Complete the structure so that the sandbags at the top are just at final water level.*

4 *Fill the lower part of the island, where the plant roots are unlikely to penetrate, with hardcore.*

5 *Top up the central part of the island with suitable compost. Aquatic planting compost is the best medium to use.*

6 *Plant towards the edge of the island using trailing plants that will hang over the side and disguise the sandbags. Space these equally around the edge.*

7 *Fill the center of the planting area with taller plants. Avoid invasive species which will crowd the center.*

Above: *A wet island is most appropriate for an informal pond; whether artificial or naturally occurring, it is a pleasing addition.*

8 *A tastefully planted island. Such features require replanting every second year if they are to retain their character.*

PLANTING SUGGESTIONS

Plants Used

Carex pendula/summer/marginal
Cotula coronopifolia/summer/marginal
Lysimachia congestifolia 'Outback Sunset'/summer/bog
Mentha aquatica/summer/marginal
Mimulus x hybridus/summer/marginal
Preslia cervina/summer/marginal

Alternative Plants

Caltha palustris 'Flore Pleno'/spring/marginal
Houttuynia cordata/summer/marginal
Iris ensata/summer/bog
Iris sibirica/summer/bog
Lysimachia nummularia/summer/marginal

making a dry brick island

The simplest island to construct for the formal pool is one made of brick. Such construction need not be regimental and mathematical, although in practice it is easier to construct and visually most appealing if built in a square or rectangular shape. The other advantage of a brick island over any other form of construction is that it can be built as a dry island. That is one where the planting area within is drier than the marginal shelves or bog garden around the pond.

The bricks are laid in a conventional fashion to create a box-like effect, the lower layer being laid on fleece underlay positioned on top of the liner. When the island's position is known well in advance, a solid slab or foundation can be positioned beneath the pond liner as the feature is being built to provide a secure base.

A brick island has to be relatively tall to stand above the water and this quite naturally leaves a cavernous space within. However, it does not have to be totally filled with soil or compost, although many gardeners prefer to do so. The bottom half or third can consist of hardcore. If you want to make sure that the island is impermeable to seepage through the bricks, a membrane can then be placed on top of this and then brought up the sides as an inner liner.

In most cases the island can be left to its own devices, the water lapping to the top of the brickwork. However, in the case of a dry island it is important that the top course of brickwork is above water level. This can often look ugly, in which case screw a plank of timber or a deck-board to the top layer of bricks. This produces a most attractive and quite natural finish.

BUILDING A BRICK ISLAND

1 *When a brick structure is built in a lined pool, it is a wise precaution to install a support slab beneath the liner.*

2 *Lay a generous bed of mortar for the first layer of bricks and ensure that they are both square and level.*

3 *The ends of the bricks must be 'buttered' with mortar to fill the gaps between them.*

4 *Lay the bricks in an alternate arrangement and ensure that each layer is level, square and vertical.*

5 *Once the mortar has dried thoroughly, a waterproofing sealant can be applied to the inner surfaces.*

6 *Fill the lower third of the structure with hardcore or gravel to provide drainage. Then top up with soil.*

7 *Choose suitable garden plants of varying flowering periods and plant as in the open garden. Here a shrub provides the focus.*

8 *A heavily planted dry island benefits from regular annual lifting and replanting.*

----- **PLANTING SUGGESTIONS** -----

Plants Used

Allium karataviense/summer/bulb
Armeria maritima 'Vesuvius'/
    summer/herbaceous
Genista lydia/spring/shrub
Saxifraga umbrosa/spring/herbaceous

Alternative Plants

Allium 'Purple Sensation'/summer/bulb
Alyssum saxatile/spring/herbaceous
Cytisus praecox 'All Gold'/spring/shrub
Dianthus 'Doris'/summer/herbaceous

Above: *A dry island enables plants that are not usually associated with water to be employed in creating imaginative designs.*

Even sizable garden trees can be included provided that they do not have root systems, which will damage the island structure.

edging with stone

The most difficult element to get right is the pond edge. Doing it correctly can certainly make the feature, while getting it wrong will ruin it completely. Whether the pond is formal or informal, the edging used is ultimately a matter of personal choice. It is certainly more usual to use paving stones for a formal feature and a stone-led planted edge for an informal one, but there are no unbreakable rules. Materials should be used that suit personal tastes and practical circumstances.

Edging is quite clearly visible and defines the pool. Wherever possible it should overhang slightly in order to protect the liner when a pond is of this construction. It should also be arranged to disguise the ungainly plastic or fiberglass edge of a preformed pond. The other important

Below: Various stones are among the most satisfactory of edges for a natural pool. Awkward edges can be easily disguised, and the use of stones as a beach is of benefit to bathing birds and wildlife.

consideration is to make the edge very stable, especially if it is an area which will be walked upon.

Where stones are used as opposed to regular paving, they should be selected not only for their beauty, but also for their resistance to extreme weather. This is especially important if they come in contact with the water, for many sandstones and some limestones shale or crumble when they are saturated with water and then frozen in winter.

Although real stone is always deemed to be most desirable, nowadays there are very convincing reconstituted stone products that are easier to use. Not only are they of uniform or consistently variable shape and size, but also of a stable structure. Thus when having to cut them to fit particular circumstances, there is little chance of them splitting and shaling in unexpected directions.

Above: *When using stone slabs, ensure that there is an overhang at the pond edge. This disguises the area where pond meets garden and reduces the effect of sunlight on an otherwise exposed liner.*

Above right: *The use of large stones to create the effect of a mountain pool works well when there is sufficient space for bold planting. This pool combines modern pavers with ancient rocks.*

edging with paving stones

Edging with stones, slabs and bricks looks most effective around a formal pond. Such edging can be applied to informal ponds, but it is much more difficult to create a convincing effect. With square, rectangular and circular ponds, however, it is very attractive.

As with most other aspects of construction, it is sensible to work out the requirements for all the elements from the beginning. There is nothing more irritating than to construct a pond, only to find when the paving comes to be laid that one slab has to be cut on each side in order to finish the edging evenly, when a simple measurement before the excavation of the pond began would have resolved the problem.

Levels are also important. The pool should be level from side to side and end to end, the surrounding land having also been leveled in order to accommodate the paving. When laid, the slabs or bricks should also be level from side to side and end to end if the finished result is to be both functional and be satisfying visually. Remember to leave sufficient width of liner around the margins of the pool so that the paving stones can anchor the liner securely. It is a good idea to allow for a small overhang over the edge of the pool to disguise the point where the liner overlaps the surrounding soil.

With stones, pavers and bricks, safety is very important. A loose slab can tip an unwary visitor into the pond, so sufficient mortar of suitable strength must be used to ensure that the slabs or bricks are bedded down securely. There are also dangers with mortar of polluting the water, as escaping lime or cement can cause eye irritation in fish. So work carefully and consider using small strips of cardboard or wood as shuttering to prevent the cement used either as the foundation or as pointing from slipping into the pool until it dries and becomes hard.

PAVING PATTERNS

Basket Weave *One of the simplest layouts and very effective when paving of a single color is used. For a more dramatic effect, use pavers of two different colors.*

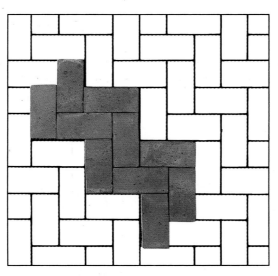

90° Herringbone *An arrangement which can be used for formal edging situations. It can look very effective with contrasting colored paving stones set around it.*

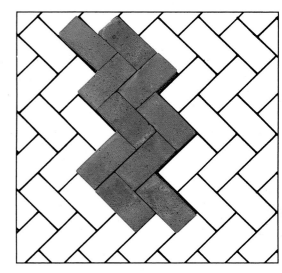

45° Herringbone *A quite complex arrangement which is best executed in paving stones of contrasting colors. It is difficult to accommodate to a pool edge.*

Left: *A formal pond is clearly defined by a paving stone edging. It is simple to create a straight edge for a square pond, but a circular one needs a little more inventiveness or the purchase of paving stones, which have curved edges. These are now quite readily available.*

EDGING A POOL WITH PAVERS

1 *Lay a generous even bed of mortar close to the edge of the pool for securing the paving.*

2 *Lay the paving stones on the mortar bed with a slight overhang. This neatens the edge.*

3 *The second row of paving stones can be used to secure the edge of the liner in position.*

4 *Cut off any surplus liner and firm the second row of paving securely on the mortar bed.*

5 *Brush a dry mortar mix into the joints between the paving stones, taking care not to let any drop into the pond. Water gently to ensure that it will set properly.*

6 *When the edge is complete, wash off any mortar splashes. Tie the water feature to the garden landscape by using cobblestones or laying turf up to the paving stone edging.*

edging with a cobble beach

With the popularity of wildlife ponds, the cobble beach has come into its own. It is not only seen as a method of edging the pond attractively, but also as providing a ready access for wildlife, especially birds, to enjoy the watery world. It also serves as an exit for small animals which might fall into the pond, but which can then clamber to safety.

An effective method of constructing a beach is firstly to excavate a shallow, sloping incline at one of the margins of the pond. The liner should be stretched over this area and then secured, either by lifting the surrounding soil or turf and tucking the liner underneath, or by trapping it between two rows of bricks or stones. If the beach is not just for birds and is going to take some pressure from foot traffic, then a shallow concrete footing can be made to trap the liner. This should be continuous for the length of the beach and immovable.

Where bricks are being used, the liner should be pulled tight and secured. The area in front and behind the bricks or footing can then be covered with cobbles to create an informal look, and this arrangement of stones then extended to the water's edge. Of all the methods of edging, the beach is the cheapest and also one of the most appealing, but remember that it is not suitable for heavy foot traffic.

While cobbles are the easiest objects to use to create a beach which looks natural, there are many other materials that can be used in their place. Shells, both natural and colored, along with smoothed colored glass chips or marbles, can also be successfully used. Even sharp sand can be employed. However, although this looks good at first, it does tend to grow a film of algae and requires constant disturbance by brushing or raking if it is to retain its attractiveness.

Above: *A cobble and slate beach is a very neat way of finishing the edge of an informal pond. Carefully constructed, it provides easy access for wildlife to drink and bathe, and is also home to all sorts of aquatic insect life.*

CREATING A COBBLE BEACH

1 Secure the liner with turf or an edge of bricks. This is essential and provides a solid base upon which the beach is constructed.

2 It is generally advisable to lay at least two rows of bricks or stones. The liner can be trapped in place between them.

3 Once the mortar has set, cobbles can be added, the larger ones being positioned first and covering the bricks.

4 A mixture of well-washed pebbles and cobbles can then be added and heaped up to a depth of 6-8 in. (15 to 20 cm).

5 To prevent cobbles rolling into the bottom of the pool, create a barrier using larger stones. These will be totally submerged.

Above: A cobble beach provides a natural and easily maintained transition from lawn to pond. It is not only practical and easy to maintain but visually very appealing.

edging with timber

Timber is a natural edging, but is not always one that fits best with a natural pond, since its most common use is in providing good secure straight edges to formal features where it can be easily fastened with screws or bolts. Properly treated timber used in this fashion is inexpensive and quite long-lasting, although it does not have the durability of stone.

Raw timber with its bark intact is often used to great effect out of the water in those areas where a bog or marsh garden is being established. Here it provides an informal and natural surround for the bog garden or for pockets of

Below: Timber can be used in a variety of ways in the water garden, from simple edging to providing a surround to a hot tub, as seen here.

planting which extend out from the pond. It is unsuitable for use beneath the water, but will serve as a water garden edging for many years, often developing its own colonies of saprophytic fungi and other interesting wild flora.

Log roll is also a useful edging, especially in a formal situation. Extensively used in many guises in the garden from path edging to creating a raised bed, it is especially effective when used both to edge the pond and to create marginal planting areas lower down in the water. Consisting of short lengths of prepared and treated round or half-round timber fastened with galvanized wire, log roll

Above: Provided that it is properly treated, timber can be used extensively in the water garden, both to edge a pond and as the main structural material, as is the case with these linked raised pools created from sleepers. It is best employed in formal situations and is one of the easiest materials for the practical home gardener to use.

has great flexibility of form and is capable of being arranged in both simple formal, as well as complex informal, configurations. A similar effect can be achieved with the use of short lengths of large-diameter bamboo drilled and bound with tarred rope. This creates a very special Oriental effect.

natural edging with plants

While timber and stone unquestionably provide the widest range of opportunities for creating imaginative pool edging, there are other methods which are visually appealing and often more appropriate.

One of the simplest and most effective is the raised beach. Primarily used for providing access for wildlife to more natural water features, it can be used most effectively in a formal situation, especially when carefully selected cobbles of uniform color are used in association with grass or planted margins.

Grass edging is also appropriate for all kinds of ponds. It can produce a clear-cut straight edge for a formal pond or tumble over the edge into an informal feature. However, it is not without its problems when it comes to maintenance, since it is important that grass cuttings do not enter the water, where they will decompose. Happily, this is not impossible to control and the resultant contrast between grass and water is worth the little extra effort that is necessary to care for the edges regularly.

Planted edges are also important, although many gardeners do not regard plants as edging as such. This is a pity because the correct choice of plants with all the right functional qualities, which at the same time are pleasing to the eye and appropriate at the waterside, can create the most effective edging of all. They should be mat-forming species and varieties of tumbling growth, ideally evergreen or partly so and with an ability to prosper in moist soil but at the same time not resent occasional inundation. The archetypal plant of this type is brooklime, *Veronica beccabunga*.

Below: *Plants are particularly convincing when planted among poolside stones and rocks. The beautifully tended lawn running to the water's edge creates a wonderful effect.*

Left: *Plants can be used freely for edging a pond provided that the water depths are compatible. With natural plantings in an earth-bottomed pond, the edges can be defined by soil sculpting – the plants only advance as far as the water depth permits.*

Below: *Strong plantings of a single variety such as irises are essential to create a bold effect for large open spaces of water. Well-planned soil sculpting before planting will confine the irises to the desired area and their tightly knit roots will form an erosion-proof edge to the water feature.*

using natural grass edging

Grass can be a most effective natural edging and, although it does present a few minor maintenance problems, it is well worth considering in a natural setting. The important consideration with a traditional turf edging is the depth of soil required up to the edge of the pond to maintain the health of the grass.

To ensure that grass edging does not dry out, it is necessary to have a minimum depth of 2 in. (5 cm) of soil, although 4 in. (10 cm) is preferable. There is nothing worse than a bright green summer lawn rolling out to a water garden where the grass immediately adjacent the pool edge is yellow or parched through lack of moisture.

If the edge is carefully arranged and the grass laid as turf, then this can be put in contact with the water which by capillary action spreads up and through the sward. It will

soak up quite an amount of water during hot summer weather and so care will be needed to ensure that the pool is regularly topped up to maintain the required water level to keep the grass healthy. Where this is successful, another problem sometimes follows: vigorous uncontrolled growth, especially of grass roots that dangle down into the pond all around the margins.

This can be overcome by using a specially selected turf that will grow and prosper on rockwool (mineral wool). This is an inert material widely used for soilless plant culture, and when used as a pool edging it is neat, clean cut and very successful in containing the spread of root growth. While horticultural rockwool of a high quality is to be preferred, household rockwool used by the building industry for roof insulation has proved to be quite satisfactory also.

TURF AND ROCKWOOL EDGING

Right: *Grass is a pleasing edging medium for a water garden, but it rapidly grows out of control and creates maintenance problems by invading the margins.*

1 *The use of good quality turf, especially of non-rhizomatous grasses, along with rockwool can ensure a permanently tidy edge to the pond.*

2 *Lift and remove the matted roots of overgrown turf. Cut back to 12 in. (30 cm.) beyond the edge.*

3 *Excavate so that a section of rockwool of the dimensions of the turf can be inserted.*

4 *Ensure that the new turf can be laid on the rockwool and then water it thoroughly.*

5 *Lay the new turf on the dampened rockwool ensuring a neat edge at the poolside.*

6 *Water the turf thoroughly. You must do this regularly until the turf and rockwool knit together. This usually takes a month or more. An occasional weak liquid feed is invaluable.*

7 *The rockwool will act as a sponge if in contact with the water. When the turf does not touch the water, weekly watering of the edge is advisable to maintain an attractive green sward.*

ornaments and decorations

The opportunities for using ornaments in a water garden are legion. Nowadays there is an industry in manufacturing everything from classical nymphs or water carriers to specially toughened mirrors or stainless steel abstract sculptures.

Beauty is in the eye of the beholder, but sometimes one has to question some of the weird timber, steel and glass creations that are installed in modern water gardens. Provided that the pond is clear-cut and formal, such flights of the imagination can work, but for the majority of gardeners designs of a more classical nature still tend to be preferred.

Ornaments used in water gardening are often associated with the movement of water, either as items in which fountains are incorporated or linked with cascades or chutes. Often this is the best way to enjoy ornaments in a water garden setting, especially if they can be enhanced by lighting.

Ornaments should not be afterthoughts. Just as the planting has to be considered carefully in order to create an overall balance, allowing for various depths and zones, so the introduction of an ornament should also be considered carefully from the outset, especially with regard to its placement.

Unlike ornaments that are used in beds, borders or as focal points in the main garden, there is another aspect to consider when decorative objects are used in or beside water. Water in all its moods and reflectiveness can have a profound effect upon the visual character of an ornament. Whenever possible, take into account the ever-changing nature of water itself when planning how you may introduce an ornament into your waterscape.

Right: *There are countless opportunities for the use of ornaments and decorations with a water garden. Here a wide combination of decorative effects is exploited, from the ornamentation within the structure of the mosaic pond itself to associated watery artifacts like shells and starfish, and the use of mirrors which give the impression of being windows to a garden beyond the blue wall. Water clarity is of vital importance here but it will be impossible to achieve by natural means. Water changes will be needed to keep such a feature looking good all year round.*

Left: *Straight lines and clearly defined angles emphasize the simplicity of this modern water feature. Uncluttered by planting, it makes a strong statement which is highlighted by the sinuous sculpture. Decoration need not be fussy – equally pleasing effects can be achieved by a single well-placed piece like this, which provides a striking focal point.*

cultivating aquatic plants

For most water gardens plants are essential, not only for their decorative value, but to create and maintain a naturally balanced eco-system. Only in very formal arrangements, especially where there is fast-flowing water, are they commonly omitted, for apart from most marginal aquatics and a few submerged plants, the remainder dislike movement in the water.

This particularly applies to waterlilies, natural inhabitants of quiet backwaters, which also object to the constant spray produced by a fountain. Available in most colors and shades, these beautiful plants with their starry blossoms are the centerpiece of most water gardens.

Deep-water aquatics inhabit the greater depths of the pond along with submerged plants, those often dull, but essential, components of the well-balanced water feature. Floating aquatics also contribute to the well-being of the pool while the marginal plants provide color and interest at the waterside. Where there is an opportunity, moisture-loving bog garden plants can be grown, extending the feature further into the conventional garden.

All aquatic plants are easily grown, although waterlilies, deep-water aquatics, marginal and submerged plants are best established and maintained in containers for ease of management. Their care is simple when grown in a well-balanced compost, and often all that is required in the way of routine care is just periodic spring division and regular manicuring during the growing season. Irrespective of the size of your water garden, from a tub on a terrace to the open water of a lake, there are plants to satisfy all your needs.

Candelabra primulas produce a glorious blaze of color at the water's edge.

pygmy and small waterlilies

While most gardeners are familiar with traditional waterlilies that grow in garden pools, there is also a range of pygmy and small-growing varieties that can be grown in tubs, containers and sinks. These can all be cultivated in the larger pond as well, providing the depth is suitable, true pygmy kinds often occupying positions on the marginal shelves.

The small-growing varieties of our familiar waterlilies have the same life-style as the larger kinds. However, the pygmy varieties can be treated differently. While most waterlilies require constant emersion in water in order to grow and prosper, the pygmy kinds can be removed and stored in damp conditions for the winter. This means that a tub which accommodates a pygmy waterlily all summer need not remain as a container full of water for the inactive six months of each year. Water can be drained from the tub and the waterlily kept damp in its compost until the spring, when water is added and once again it grows away strongly.

Pygmy waterlilies can also be grown very successfully in rock pools providing that there is no water flowing through them. As winter approaches, drain off the pool, fill it with straw and cover tightly with Plexiglas™ or ployethylene. The waterlilies will overwinter well and the risk of damage to the rock pool from the small body of water freezing solid and expanding will be eliminated. If this is considered unsightly, a pool heater will prevent severe freezing.

Above: *Pygmy waterlilies are complete miniature replicas of standard varieties. They have the same flowering season, which extends from early summer until autumn.*

***

CULTIVATION TIPS

Pygmy and small-growing varieties of waterlilies are grown in containers or baskets, although sometimes the pygmy kinds are planted directly into suitable soil or an aquatic planting compost on the bottom of small tub or planter where space is restricted.

They are all easygoing, requiring repotting and replanting every three years and fertilizing regularly during the seasons between.

Below: Nymphaea *'Pygmaea Helvola' is very prolific.*

RECOMMENDED VARIETIES

Nymphaea 'Graziella'
Orange-red flowers up to 2 in. (5 cm) across with deep orange stamens are produced in abundance throughout the summer. The olive-green leaves are blotched with brown and purple. Spread: 1-2 ft. (30-60 cm). Depth: 1-2 ft. (30-60 cm). Flowering period: summer. Propagation: eyes.

N. 'Hermine'
Tulip-shaped blossoms of the purest white are held above the dark green oval foliage. Spread: 1-2 ft. (30-60 cm). Depth: 1-2 ft. (30-60 cm). Flowering period: summer. Propagation: eyes.

N. 'Nymphaea Odorata Pumila'
A hardy waterlily with leathery, glossy green leaves. The day-blooming flower is white, cup-shaped and fragrant. Spread: 8 in. (20 cm) Depth: 8 in. (20 cm). Flowering period: summer. Propagation: eyes.

N. 'Pygmaea Helvola'
Beautiful star-like canary-yellow flowers are produced throughout the summer among olive green foliage which is heavily mottled with purple and brown. Spread: 1 foot (30 cm). Depth: up to 1 foot (30 cm). Flowering period: summer. Propagation: eyes.

N. 'William Falconer'
Blood red flowers with bright yellow stamens are produced among deep olive green lily pads which in their early stages of growth are a distinctive purplish hue. Spread: 1½-2 ft. (45-60 cm). Depth: 1½-2 ft. (45-60 cm). Flowering period: summer. Propagation: eyes.

Above: *All waterlilies must have full uninterrupted sunlight if they are to prosper. With pygmy and small-growing varieties, it is important to top up the pool or container regularly with water to replace that lost to evaporation. Neglecting to do this will result in a rapid deterioration of the plants.*

'PROBLEM' VARIETIES
While white and yellow pygmy waterlilies are free-flowering and well worth growing, the red ones are a big disappointment. *Nymphaea* 'Pygmaea Rubra' and *N.* 'Pygmaea Rubis' produce small numbers of flowers and very few manage to come out at the same time. Both varieties are difficult to propagate as they produce eyes sparingly. The few flowers that these varieties produce are sterile and so seed is not an option.

medium-sized waterlilies

There is a wonderful array of waterlilies available for the gardener with the average-sized garden pond. The much-loved older varieties were produced in France during the latter part of the 19th century and the early part of the 20th century. All have a long history of cultivation and are reliable in most climates.

Waterlilies are available in a wide range of colors, only blue and smoky green being found in tropical varieties but not among the hardies. Flower shapes vary from star-like in 'Rose Arey' to peony-shaped with 'James Brydon' and cup-shaped with 'Marliacea Albida.' Unlike the tropical varieties which raise their flowers above the water, most of those of the hardy kinds float on the surface of the water among the waterlily pads.

All the medium-sized waterlilies popularly offered for sale are completely winter hardy. Their size varies according to the depth at which they are growing, the shallower the water the smaller the surface spread of foliage.

The greatest diversity of flower shapes, color, fragrance and leaf patterns are to be found among the older, more traditional medium-sized varieties of waterlily.

Above: *Nymphaea 'James Brydon' is the best peony-shaped flowered waterlily available, although it does take a season to settle down into a regular flowering pattern.*

RECOMMENDED VARIETIES

Nymphaea 'Arc-en-ciel'

The only truly variegated foliage variety of waterlily. The leaves are deep olive green boldly splashed with purple, rose, white and bronze. The flowers have narrow petals and are pink and papery. Spread: 1½-3 ft. (45-90 cm). Depth: 1½-3 ft. (45-90 cm). Flowering period: summer. Propagation: eyes.

N. 'Gloire de Temple-sur-Lot'

A fully double, fragrant, rose-pink flowered waterlily which has the appearance of a chrysanthemum rather than a waterlily. Large plain green leaves.
Spread: 1½-3 ft. (45-90 cm). Depth: 1½-3 ft. (45-90 cm). Flowering period: summer. Propagation: eyes.

N. 'James Brydon'

A wonderful crimson-flowered waterlily with rounded blossoms rather like those of a peony. Dark purplish-green leaves which are often flecked with maroon.
Spread: 1½-3 ft. (45-90 cm). Depth: 1½-3 ft. (45-90 cm). Flowering period: summer. Propagation: eyes.

N. 'Marliacea Albida'

Fragrant pure white cup-shaped blossoms up to 6 in. (15 cm) across. The sepals and reverse of the petals are often flushed with pink. The leaves are dark green with purplish undersides. Spread: 1½-3 ft. (45-90 cm). Depth: 1½-3 ft. (45-90 cm). Flowering period: summer. Propagation: eyes.

N. 'Marliacea Chromatella'

Large canary yellow blossoms with broad petals. The sepals are pale yellow and flushed with pink. The olive green foliage is distinctively splashed and stained with maroon and bronze. Spread: 1½-2½ ft. (45-75 cm). Depth: 1½-2½ ft. (45-75 cm). Flowering period: summer. Propagation: eyes.

N. 'Rose Arey'

Large star-like rose-pink blossoms with a wonderful aniseed fragrance. The juvenile leaves are red and the adult green leaves often have a distinctive reddish flush.
Spread: 1½-2½ ft. (45-75 cm). Depth: 1½-2½ ft. (45-75 cm). Flowering period: summer. Propagation: eyes.

Above: Nymphaea odorata *'Alba' is a very hardy and free-flowering fragrant waterlily variety with attractive apple-green foliage.*

·········· 'PROBLEM' VARIETIES ··········

There is only one medium-sized waterlily to avoid and that is *N.* 'Col. A.J. Welch.' This is a sparsely flowered yellow variety which reproduces viviparously. Often what appears to be a promising bud turns out to be a plantlet. As it reproduces so freely, it is often offered cheaply in garden centers. It is in any event a rather vigorous and coarse-growing variety with an excess of foliage.

Left: Nymphaea *'Marliacea Chromatella' is a most reliable and free-flowering waterlily for the medium-sized pool. It is very versatile and will continue to prosper in as little as 1 foot (30 cm) of water or as much as 40 in. (1 meter), which is why it is so widely available from garden centers.*

large waterlilies

There are a number of magnificent large waterlilies which are only well suited to the farm pond or lake. For most gardeners the cultivation of these beautiful aquatics is out of the question, but it is important to know which varieties are suited to large expanses of water as they are often offered for sale to home gardeners for average-sized garden pools. They will grow in shallower water of course, but the flowers and foliage will not develop to the full.

Large-growing waterlilies are not very suitable for cultivating in baskets. They are much too vigorous. They grow much more freely when allowed to roam around the pool floor. When growing happily, varieties like *N.* 'Gladstone' and *N.* 'Escarboucle' can produce spectacular blossoms up to 10 in. (25 cm) across and individual lily pads as much as 1 foot (30 cm) in diameter. When growing these giants allow between 6½ ft. (2 m) and 10 ft. (3 m) of surface area to be covered by the foliage of each plant. None will grow freely in less than 4 ft. (1.2 m) of water.

Below: Of the various strong-growing purple and plum-colored varieties with white streaking, it is Nymphaea *'Charles de Meurville' which has the longest flowering season.*

···· **RECOMMENDED VARIETIES** ····

Nymphaea 'Charles de Meurville'

A vigorous grower with large plum-colored blossoms, the petals of which are tipped and streaked with white. The flowers darken to deep wine with age. The foliage is deep olive green. Spread: 4-6 ft. (1.2-1.8 m). Depth: 4-6 ft. (1.2-1.8 m). Flowering period: summer. Propagation: eyes.

N. 'Escarboucle'

A very large-flowered, richly fragrant crimson variety with a center of bright yellow stamens. Immense bright green lily pads. Spread: 4-6 ft. (1.2-1.8 m). Depth: 4-6 ft. (1.2-1.8 m). Flowering period: summer. Propagation: eyes.

N. 'Gladstone'

Enormous pure white waxy blossoms with centers of bold yellow stamens. Dark green leaves with leaf stalks speckled brown. Spread: 4-8 ft. (1.2-2.4 m). Depth: 4-8 ft. (1.2-2.4 m). Flowering period: summer. Propagation: eyes.

N. 'Marliacea Carnea'

Flesh-pink vanilla-scented blossoms with bright yellow stamens are produced in abundance among plain green foliage which is often purplish when it first emerges. Newly planted specimens sometimes produce white flowers during the first season. Spread: 4-6 ft. (1.2-1.8 m). Depth: 4-6 ft. (1.2-1.8 m). Flowering period: summer. Propagation: eyes.

N. Nymphaea 'Gonnère'

Light green, rounded foliage contrasts with layers of broad petals nested, star-like, within one another and measuring 4-6 in. (10-15 cm) across. Young foliage is bronzed. Spread: 3-4 ft. (90 cm-1.2 m). Depth: 3-4 ft. (90 cm-1.2 m).

Above: Nymphaea *'Escarboucle' is one of the most versatile large-growing waterlilies. When given an unrestricted root run and a generous depth of water, it proves itself to be truly the queen of aquatics, with individual blossoms the size of soup plates.*

Left: Nymphaea *'Marliacea Carnea' is probably the most widely cultivated pink flowered waterlily. Raised by the famous French hybridizer Joseph Bory Latour Marliac, it is also erroneously sold under the name of 'Morning Glory.'*

other deep-water aquatics

While the deeper area of the pool unquestionably belongs to the waterlilies, there are occasions when the introduction of other deep-water aquatics can be of great benefit. The two most valuable attributes of those plants referred to by nursery staff as deep-water aquatics are their tolerance of moving water and seasonality of display.

Unless the pool is very large it is impossible to grow a waterlily successfully when either a fountain or waterfall is introduced. Waterlilies are natural inhabitants of quiet backwaters and go into a rapid decline when subjected to water flow or constant splashing on the foliage. The nuphars

Above: The water hawthorn, Aponogeton distachyos, *is not only a floral delight, but a culinary delicacy. The crispy white flowers are an excellent addition to salads.*

or pond lilies can take their place, being tolerant of both moving water and a little shade. They produce floating foliage that is very similar to a waterlily, but one has to concede that the flowers are not as spectacular.

With the water hawthorn, *Aponogeton distachyos*, the foliage is smaller and not as effective, but the vanilla-scented blossoms are superb.

Aponogeton distachyos (Water hawthorn)

The blossoms are forked white with black stamens, and have a delicious vanilla fragrance. The more or less oblong green leaves are often splashed with maroon. Spread: 1-3 ft. (30-90 cm). Depth: 1-3 ft. (30-90 cm). Flowering period: late spring to winter. Propagation: division/seed.

Nuphar advena (American spatterdock)

A strong-growing pond lily with globular yellow blossoms 3 in. (8 cm) across. These are often tinged with purple and have bright coppery-red stamens. The large fresh green lily pads are thick and leathery. Spread: 1½-5 ft. (45 cm-1.5 m). Depth: 1½-5 ft. (45 cm-1.5 m). Flowering period: summer. Propagation: division.

N. lutea (Yellow pond lily)

Small bottle-shaped yellow flowers with a distinctive alcoholic aroma are produced among leathery fresh green oval leaves. A vigorous plant which is best suited to the larger pool. Spread: 1-8 ft. (30 cm-2.4 m). Depth: 1-8 ft. (30 cm-2.4 m). Flowering period: summer. Propagation: division.

Orontium aquaticum (Golden club)

A curious relative of the arum lily which produces masses of upright pencil-like blossoms in bright gold and white. The blue-green foliage is lance-shaped and floats on the surface of the water.
Spread: 1½ ft. (45 cm.). Depth: up to 1½ ft. (45 cm). Flowering period: summer.
Propagation: division.

Opposite page: Nymphoides peltata *is a very adaptable but invasive plant that is prohibited from sale in some states.*

Above: Orontium aquaticum *is among the hardiest and finest free-flowering deep-water aquatics.*

reeds and rushes

After waterlilies, most people would regard reeds and rushes as the next most typical plants of a pond. Especially popular are the typhas or reedmaces, with their thick chocolate-colored fruiting spikes which are popularly referred to as bulrushes.

Reeds and rushes are among the most difficult plants to grow successfully in a garden pool. Most are not too fond of cultivation in a basket unless kept well fertilized.

Below: The poker-like heads of the lesser reedmace, Typha angustifolia, *are much admired. However, the plant is very invasive and must be contained within a planting basket or restricted by water depth when planted directly into the margins.*

If let loose in the soil on the margins of a pool they spread rapidly and grow into one another. Providing that their behavior is well understood, however, they can be satisfactorily cultivated and make a major contribution to the visual aspect of a pool.

All have architectural qualities, which in the case of the *Juncus* or true rushes persist all year long. The scirpus or *Schoenoplectus* are almost evergreen too and add much with their often startlingly bold foliage. Flowers are the least important characteristic of most reeds and rushes, except for the flowering rush, *Butomus umbellatus*, which in late summer produces pink blossoms. Invasive, it is prohibited for sale in some states.

Right: Sweet galingale, Cyperus longus, *is happiest when established on a bank and allowed to colonize mud at the water's edge.*

Carex pendula (Pendulous sedge)

One of the few sedges which are worth growing in the pool. A tall handsome plant with broad green strap-like leaves and long drooping brownish-green catkin-like flowers during summer. Height: 3-4 ft. (90 cm-1.2 m). Spread: 1½-2 ft. (45-60 cm). Depth up to 4 in. (10 cm). Flowering period: summer. Propagation: division/seed.

Juncus effusus 'Spiralis' (Corkscrew rush)

A bizarre version of the common soft rush but with dark green needle-like leaves which are twisted and contorted like a corkscrew. A great novelty which produces small brown tassels of flowers. Height: 1-1½ ft. (30-45 cm). Spread 6-10 in. (15-25 cm). Depth: up to 6 in. (15 cm). Flowering period: summer. Propagation: division.

Schoenoplectus tabernaemontani 'Zebrinus' (Zebra rush)

A startling mutant plant with thick long needle-like stems which are alternately banded horizontally with white and green. Occasional small tassels of brown flowers are produced. Height: 3-4 ft. (90 cm-1.2 m). Spread: 1½-2 ft. (45-60 cm). Depth: up to 6 in. (15 cm). Flowering period: summer. Propagation: division.

Typha minima (Dwarf Japanese bulrush)

This wonderful dwarf rush produces masses of dark green needle-like foliage among which chunky rounded brown fruiting heads are produced. Height: 18 in. (45 cm). Spread: 6-8 in. (15-20 cm). Depth: up to 4 in. (10 cm). Flowering period: summer. Propagation: division.

Below: *Reeds and rushes make an important visual and functional contribution to the pool and provide a wonderful habitat for wildlife.*

'PROBLEM' VARIETIES

Avoid all species of plain green *Juncus*, *Carex* and the smaller leaf *Schoenoplectus*. These are weedy species which seed themselves freely and can swamp a pond. A number, such as *Juncus effusus* and *Carex riparia*, are offered by nurseries and garden centers for wildlife ponds, but they should be avoided as they can become really pernicious and create serious maintenance problems.

irises

Of all the marginal plants it is the irises that show the richest diversity. They are of varying stature and have flowers of almost every color and combination imaginable. Outside the pond the iris family is extraordinary with tiny bulbous species for the rock garden, monster bearded kinds for the sunny herbaceous border and elegant moisture-loving varieties for the bog garden. It is the moisture-loving kind that are sometimes confused with the true water iris, since there are great similarities in appearance and not all nurseries or garden centers know the difference.

There is a simple test which the gardener can carry out to determine whether an iris will be happy in the margins of a pond or prefer life in a bog garden. Take an iris leaf between the index finger and thumb and run gently up the leaf. If the leaf is smooth, the iris will be happy standing in water. If the leaf has a strong mid-rib, then it will prefer to inhabit a bog garden.

Irises are principally grown for their beautiful blossoms which are produced freely during mid-summer, but their bold sword-like foliage can be magnificent, particularly the variegated varieties, and produce quite dramatic architectural effects, especially in the formal pool.

Left: *Yellow flag,* Iris pseudacorus, *is a marvelous plant for the larger pool or wildlife pond. It has yielded many good varieties. Apart from the creamy-yellow and green variegated 'Variegata,' there is a double-flowered form 'Flore Pleno,' a pale yellow variety 'Sulfur Queen,' as well as the creamy-white flowered 'E. Turnipseed.'*

Right: *Irises of all kinds, irrespective of whether they are true aquatics or bog varieties, offer great opportunities for imaginative use by the water gardener.*

Iris laevigata

The parent of many of the brightly colored aquatic iris. A handsome blue flowered plant with bold clumps of smooth green sword-like foliage. Height: 2-3 ft. (60-90 cm). Spread: 1-1½ ft. (30-45 cm). Depth: up to 6 in. (15 cm). Flowering period: summer. Propagation: division/seed.

I. laevigata 'Variegata'

This plant is often sold under the name of 'Elegantissima.' It has the same beautiful blue flowers as its parent and spectacular green and white variegated sword-like foliage. Height: 2-2½ ft. (60-75 cm). Spread: 1-1⅓ ft. (30-40 cm). Depth up to 4 in. (10 cm). Flowering period: summer. Propagation: division.

I. pseudacorus (Yellow flag)

A very well-known vigorous-growing plant for the larger water garden and wildlife pool. Tall mid-green strap-like leaves and bright yellow blossoms with conspicuous black markings. The dark green seed pods split to reveal orange-brown seeds. Height: 3-4 ft. (90 cm-1.2 m). Spread: 1½-2 ft. (45-60 cm). Depth up to 10 in. (25 cm). Flowering period: summer. Propagation: division/seed.

I. pseudacorus 'Variegata'

One of the most spectacular variegated foliage plants. Although producing bright yellow flowers like its parent the yellow flag, it is the handsome creamy-yellow and green striped foliage for which this plant is grown. Height: 2-2½ ft. (60-75 cm). Spread: 1-1⅓ ft. (30-40 cm). Depth: up to 6 in. (15 cm). Flowering period: summer. Propagation: division.

I. versicolor 'Kermesina'

The most beautiful variety of the widely cultivated *Iris versicolor*. Deep plum-colored blossoms with golden markings. Bold green sword-like leaves. Height: 2-2½ ft. (60-75 cm). Spread: 1-1⅓ ft. (30-40 cm). Depth: up to 4 in. (10 cm). Flowering period: summer. Propagation: division.

other marginals

The poolside provides endless opportunities for growing an enormous range of interesting plants. In many cases the marginal area of the pool is devoted to plants that disguise the harsh edge and provide a seamless union to the area where garden and water meet: plants like the scrambling brooklime, *Veronica beccabunga,* creeping jenny, *Lysimachia nummularia;* or invasive water mint, *Mentha aquatica.* Such spreading characters can be punctuated with the bold foliage of the aquatic irises or dark green mounds of the marsh marigold, *Caltha palustris.*

Marginal plants can also extend the period of color and interest in a pool. Waterlilies are really only interesting for the summer months. It is characters like the common marsh marigold, *Caltha palustris*, and its double form 'Flore Pleno' which provide spring highlights at a time when the pool is devoid of plant life and offers just a glassy stillness.

The use of selected marginal aquatics also provides an opportunity for creating a successful wildlife pool, since on the confines of a marginal shelf a surprising array of interesting plants can be accommodated adjacent to one another, each with the potential to contribute to the life cycle of a different creature.

RECOMMENDED VARIETIES

Calla palustris (Bog arum)
An excellent creeping marginal for disguising the pool edge. It has a strong creeping rootstock which is clothed in handsome glossy heart-shaped foliage. The white blossoms are like small sails and are followed during late summer by bright orange-red fruits. Height: 6 in.-1 foot. (15-30 cm). Spread: 4-6 in. (10-15 cm). Depth: up to 4 in. (10 cm). Flowering period: summer. Propagation: seed/division/cuttings.

Caltha palustris (Marsh marigold)
A great marginal plant for spring flowering. Dark green mounds of glossy scalloped dark green foliage are smothered in bright golden-yellow waxy saucer-shaped blossoms. Height: 1-2 ft. (30-60 cm). Spread: 6 in.-1 foot (15-30 cm). Depth: up to 1 foot (30 cm), but best in 4 in. (10 cm) of water. Flowering period: spring. Propagation: seed/division/cuttings.

Left: Pontederia cordata *is a highlight of the late summer pool.*

···· RECOMMENDED VARIETIES ····

***Lysimachia nummularia* (Creeping jenny)** A fast-growing creeping almost evergreen plant which during summer is smothered with yellow buttercup-like flowers. Height: 1 inch (2.5 cm). Spread: 1-1½ ft. (30-45 cm). Depth: up to 4 in. (10 cm). Will grow through water without difficulty. Flowering period: summer. Propagation: division.

***Myosotis scorpioides* (Water forget-me-not)** An aquatic and perennial version of our common bedding forget-me-not, but perennial. A hummock-forming smooth-leafed plant which for most of the summer is smothered with tiny blue starry flowers. Height: 8-10 in. (20-25 cm). Spread: 4-6 in. (10-15 cm). Depth: up to 4 in. (10 cm). Flowering period: summer. Propagation: seed/division.

***Pontederia cordata* (Pickerel)** Spikes of soft blue flowers appear from among sheaves of glossy dark green leaves during late summer. A fine upright architectural plant. Height: 2-3 ft. (60-90 cm). Spread: 1-1½ ft. (30-45 cm). Depth: up to 6 in. (15 cm). Flowering period: late summer. Propagation: seed/division/cuttings.

***Veronica beccabunga* (Brooklime)** Dark blue flowers with distinctive white eyes are produced in the axils of the leaves of this fast-growing evergreen scrambling aquatic. Perfect for growing to disguise the harsh edge of an artificial pond. Height: 6-8 in. (15-20 cm). Spread: 4 in. (10 cm). Depth: up to 4 in. (10 cm). Flowering period: summer. Propagation: division.

Right: *Spring delights at the waterside with golden hummocks of* Caltha palustris *and the hooded spathes of* Lysichiton americanus.

floating and submerged plants

Many gardeners regard these as the least important pond plants, and from an aesthetic point of view they are the most uninteresting. However, both submerged and floating aquatics are the powerhouse of the pond's ecology. Without them the only way to maintain water clarity is with a pool filter, and for most aquatic life this is a sterile and wholly naked environment. The water may be pure, but without places for pondlife to hide, feed and reproduce, the pond becomes a furniture-less room.

The submerged plants are not very noticeable as they spend their lives rooted to the pool floor and only emerge above the surface of the water to flower. With the exception of the water violet, *Hottonia palustris,* and the water crowfoot, *Ranunculus aquatilis,* none of them produces attractive flowers and they make no visual contribution to the aquatic scene.

Floating plants are a similar proposition, although the white blossoms of both the invasive water chestnut, *Trapa natans* (prohibited for sale in some states), and the frogbit, *Hydrocharis morsus-ranae*, are quite pretty. It is the way in which they function together that is important – the floating plants, which reduce the light falling into the water and so lower algal activity, are complemented by the submerged plants which mop up excess nutrients that are present in the water and help to starve the algae out of existence.

FLOATING PLANTS

Hydrocharis morsus-ranae (Frogbit)

An excellent small floating plant for tub, container or small pond. Neat rosettes of mid-green kidney-shaped leaves sprinkled with three-petaled white blossoms throughout the summer.
Flowering period: summer. Propagation: division.

Utricularia vulgaris (Greater bladderwort)

Bright yellow antirrhinum-like flowers are produced on strong stems which emerge from a mass of fine green foliage which floats just beneath the surface of the water. These are interspersed with bladders which capture and digest errant aquatic insects.
Flowering period: summer. Propagation: division.

Above: *Water crowfoot,* Ranunculus aquatilis, *is one of the most attractive flowering submerged aquatics. It grows happily in both still and quickly flowing water.*

Right: *The versatile* Myriophyllum aquaticum *often takes on rich red and orange hues at the approach of autumn.*

SUBMERGED PLANTS

Hottonia palustris (Water violet)

The most beautiful of the hardy submerged aquatics. Lovely whorled bright green filigree foliage atop which during summer are produced spikes of fine whitish or lilac-flushed blossoms. Flowering period: summer. Propagation: cuttings.

Myriophyllum proserpinacoides (Parrot's feather)

A plant which can grow submerged, climb out on to the margins of the pool and even invade the bog garden. Blue-green finely cut leaves on scrambling stems. A most versatile plant. Flowering period: summer. Propagation: cuttings.

Ranunculus aquatilis (Water crowfoot)

An excellent submerged aquatic which produces beautiful papery white and gold blossoms during summer just above the water and among clover-like floating leaves. The submerged foliage is deeply dissected and much loved by fish as a place to spawn. Flowering period: summer. Propagation: cuttings.

flowering bog plants

The bog garden is a wonderful adjunct to the pool since it can offer an attractive backdrop and provide interest and color for much of the year. Even during the winter a well-placed clump of the moisture-loving, red-stemmed *Cornus alba* 'Sibirica' or a stooled specimen of the orange-stemmed willow, *Salix alba* 'Chermesina,' can create height and colorful interest.

It is the flowering bog plants that produce the most lasting and startling color, although the summer clothing of foliage on structural plants like the cornus and willow offers a wonderful backdrop and softens their harshness.

Right: Candelabra primulas and moisture-loving irises live together in tangled harmony and make a wonderful late spring and early summer display of color in the bog garden.

Far right: Bog garden plants are also adaptable to streamside planting where they may receive periodic inundation.

Left: Candelabra primulas are easily increased from seed sown immediately after it ripens. Do not allow the plants to self-seed naturally. Remove faded flower heads before seed distribution takes place.

Many bog garden plants are very brightly colored, especially the early summer-flowering primulas like the bright crimson *Primula japonica* and vivid orange *P. aurantiaca*. Equally colorful are the perennial lobelias such as *Lobelia cardinalis* with its scarlet blossoms and beet-colored foliage and *L. vedrariensis* sporting rich violet flowers and maroon-flushed leaves.

The bog garden first comes to life in early spring with the bright pink of *Primula rosea* and the lilac and white drumsticks of *P. denticulata*. Color and interest continue throughout the season until the last fading blossoms of the bright orange *Ligularia* 'Desdemona' fall with the arrival of autumn winds.

RECOMMENDED VARIETIES

Astilbe arendsii hybrids

These are a group of brightly colored mid- to late summer flowering plants with dense plumes of blossoms appearing above mounds of densely cut foliage. 'Fanal' is red, 'Peach Blossom' pink and 'Irrlicht' white. Height: 1½-3 ft. (45-90 cm). Spread: 10 in.-1½ ft. (25-45 cm). Flowering period: summer. Propagation: division.

Cardamine pratensis (Cuckoo flower)

A charming spring-flowering perennial with single rosy-lilac flowers and pale green fern-like foliage. The variety 'Flore Pleno' has fully double blossoms. Height: 1-1½ ft. (30-45 cm). Spread: 6-10 in. (15-25 cm). Flowering period: spring. Propagation: division/seed

Filipendula ulmaria (Meadowsweet)

Frothy spires of scented creamy-white blossoms are reproduced during summer above deeply cut foliage. There is a double flowered form called 'Flore Pleno' and a golden leafed one – 'Aurea.' Height: 2-4 ft. (60 cm-1.2 m). Spread: 1-2 ft. (30-60 cm). Flowering period: summer. Propagation: division/seed.

Iris ensata (Clematis-flowered iris of Japan)

The finest swamp iris. The species has tufts of grassy foliage surmounted by broad-petaled deep purple blossoms during summer. There are many named varieties in a rich array of colors. Height: 2-2½ ft. (60-75 cm). Spread: 1-1⅓ ft. (30-40 cm). Flowering period: summer. Propagation: division/seed.

Lobelia cardinalis

One of the most startling red-flowered plants. Vivid blossoms borne in spires above beet-colored foliage. There are a whole range of different colored hybrids available with both green and maroon leaves. Height: 2-3 ft. (60-90 cm). Spread: 1-1½ ft. (30-45 cm). Flowering period: summer. Propagation: division/seed.

Primula candelabra hybrids

Early summer-flowering primulas with tiered whorls of multicolored blossoms above coarse cabbagy leaves. There are a whole range of both species and named varieties in separate colors. Height: 2-2½ ft. (60-75 cm). Spread: 1-1⅓ ft. (30-40 cm). Flowering period: summer. Propagation: division/seed.

foliage bog plants

While the main attraction of a bog garden is the flowering plants, foliage subjects do make a major contribution. Not only do they provide a cool green foil for brightly colored bog plants, but they convey a feeling of luxuriance which is associated with natural waterside vegetation. Some add summer structure to the bog garden or streamside, notably the ornamental rhubarbs or rheums and stately ferns like *Osmunda regalis*, the royal fern.

Above: *The ornamental rhubarb,* Rheum palmatum tanguticum, *is a magnificent architectural plant. To retain high quality foliage, it is necessary to remove the main stems before they become towering spires of tiny blossoms.*

Left: *Hostas or plantain lilies are the best all-round foliage plants for bog garden and waterside planting. They are available in plain green, blue-green and many variegated forms.*

Among the wide diversity of foliage plants which enjoy bog garden life are many choice subjects. These include the steely gray-green hostas or plantain lilies and their startling banded and variegated varieties in green, white, cream and gold, the elegant sensitive fern, *Onoclea sensibilis*, which happily colonizes mud at the water's edge, along with the parasols of the umbrella plant, *Darmera peltata*, which during early autumn turn from bright green to bronze and coppery-red.

Much can be achieved with foliage plants by their careful placement, not only as complements to their flowering neighbors, but as important architectural plants.

Above: Ostrich feather fern, Matteuccia struthiopteris, is the finest of the bog garden ferns with its bright green shuttlecocks of foliage.

⋯⋯ RECOMMENDED VARIETIES ⋯⋯

Hosta fortunei (Plantain lily)

One of the best hostas, not only for its handsome large oval grayish-green foliage, but also its summer spikes of tubular lilac to violet flowers. It has yielded many varieties including 'Albopicta' with golden centers to the leaves, 'Aurea,' bright yellow foliage fading to green, and the gold-edged 'Aureomarginata.' Height: 2-3 ft. (60-90 cm). Spread: 2-2½ ft. (30-45 cm). Propagation: division.

Matteuccia struthiopteris (Ostrich feather fern)

Handsome bright green lacy fronds arranged like a shuttlecock around a stout woody crown. The dark-colored fertile fronds appear from the center of the crown during mid-summer. Height: 3 ft. (90 cm). Spread: 2½ ft. (45 cm). Propagation: division.

Onoclea sensibilis (Sensitive fern)

A perfect fern for the streamside with erect flattened fronds which arise from a knotted black creeping rootstock. In spring the foliage is strongly flushed with pink. Height: 1½-2 ft. (45-60 cm). Spread: 8 in.-2 ft. (20-30 cm). Propagation: division.

Osmunda regalis (Royal fern)

A stately fern with large leathery fronds which change color from pale green during early spring, through mid-green to coppery bronze in autumn. There is also a purplish form called 'Purpurascens.' Height: 4-6 ft. (1.2-1.8 m). Spread: 2-3 ft. (60-90 cm). Propagation: division.

Rheum palmatum (Ornamental rhubarb)

This great architectural plant has broad-spreading foliage like a very refined rhubarb and tall spires of tiny creamy-white blossoms. There is a purplish cut-leafed form called *tanguticum* and a deep crimson red flowered variety called 'Bowles' Crimson.' Height: 5-6 ft. (1.5-1.8 m). Spread: 2½-3 ft. (75-90 cm). Propagation: division.

choosing plants

It is always preferable to choose aquatic plants from a specialist nursery, or alternatively from a garden center that has an aquatic plant department that is stocked by a specialist grower. Ideally all marginal plants and waterlilies should be pot grown. Never purchase waterlilies or other aquatic plants which are floating loosely around in a sales tank. They will already have started to deteriorate. Bare-rooted aquatic plants are only satisfactory if received freshly lifted from the nursery.

Some garden centers and pet stores offer prepacked aquatics, particularly submerged and floating plants. If these are sealed in polyethylene and hung on a peg board, give them a wide berth. They heat up quickly and spoil.

This also happens sometimes with submerged aquatics which are stocked loose in bunches in a tank. To check whether submerged plants are likely to be a good buy, look at the lead weight around the base of the bunch of cuttings. Black marks on the stems in the vicinity of the foliage indicate that the plant has been bunched for at least a week and that the lead strip is probably causing the stems to rot at the point where they are held together. Such plants should be avoided.

1 *Bog garden plants should be well clothed with unblemished foliage.*

2 *This hosta represents good value. When removed from the pot, it will be readily divisible.*

3 *A well-grown plant should display healthy foliage and also be capable of flowering successfully.*

4 *Plants should be established in their pots and not starved.*

5 *It is important that plants are free from pests and display only healthy undamaged foliage.*

Iris

Hosta

Astilbe

Stipa

Lysimachia

Lobelia

Right: *For a garden pool to be a success, it is important to choose a range of aquatic plants which will create a harmonious balance. These plants should all have had the best possible start in life.*

Above: *These plants show good husbandry. They are all growing healthily with no signs of pests and diseases. The containers are clean and topped off with a fresh layer of gravel and all are of reliable varieties.*

Right: *All the qualities of a good plant are visible here – healthy foliage, a full-sized flower and well presented container topped with gravel.*

Left: *A plant to avoid – starved and in an inadequate container competing with a mass of seedling weeds*

soils and composts

The soil or compost that is used for growing pond plants has a considerable influence not only upon their growth and performance, but also upon the clarity of the water in the pond. Healthy aquatic plants require a balance of nutrients in order to prosper, but these have to be available in such a form that the plants can readily assimilate them, without any leaching into the water. When nutrients become freely available in the water, they can be readily used by submerged plants, and when in excess, by green water-discoloring algae too. The successful balance of a water garden depends upon the aquatic plants having a suitable medium in which to grow; there should be sufficient nutrients available for their well-being, but not for the undesirable lower forms of plant life, like slimes and algae, to prosper.

Aquatic planting composts are the most expensive growing mediums, but they do have the advantage of being balanced for successful pond plant cultivation, the nutrients being available in a slow-release form which does not readily disperse into the water. However, good clear garden soil, especially if of a medium or heavy nature, can be converted into a suitable growing medium for all aquatic plants.

Good clean garden soil is a viable alternative to aquatic planting compost. Any medium to heavy soil is suitable providing that it has not been dressed recently with artificial fertilizer. Sieve it well to remove any sticks and stones or water-polluting organic material.

SOIL TEXTURE

Below: *A balanced pond environment and healthy plants result from the use of properly prepared growing medium. There should be sufficient nutrients for the plants, without encouraging green algal bloom.*

1 *Take some heavy garden soil from a part of the garden which has not recently received fertilizer. Dry thoroughly and break it down so that it can be spooned into an empty jar. Fill to within 1 inch (2.5 cm) of the top.*

2 *Fill the jar to the top with clean tap water, allowing the dry soil particles to soak it up thoroughly. There will be considerable bubbling as the water drives out the air between the crumbs of soil.*

3 *Replace the lid and shake the jar thoroughly so that the soil particles are turned into a muddy slurry. The consistency of the contents should be like very runny chocolate, with no discernible soil crumb structure evident.*

4 *Leave the jar undisturbed and allow the contents to settle out. Sand settles first, followed by clay, then clear water with organic matter floating on the top. 50 per cent clay content is the minimum requirement for aquatic plants.*

planting and containers

It is important that pond plants have sufficient opportunity to develop a good root system without becoming over-crowded. Of all the plants that are grown in the decorative garden, aquatic plants unquestionably have the lustiest root growth. For this reason they are best grown in containers where they can be prevented from straying into one another, a particular benefit when routine division of the rootstocks takes place. Entangled neighbors can be a nightmare when the time comes to separate one from another.

Aquatic plants are unlike other garden plants since they do not grow well in ordinary plant pots. It is true that plants will prosper for a short time, but before the end of the season they will go into decline, irrespective of the compost. There needs to be an ability for the roots of the plants to escape into the water and for the compost to be effectively ventilated by direct exposure to the water through the sides of a lattice-work basket. In a closed pot, within 12 to 18 months the compost will turn blue or black and smell very unpleasant.

There are a wide range of aquatic planting baskets available, and although they are more expensive than pots or similar containers, they are an excellent investment and ensure that pond plants develop to their full potential.

Planting containers range from micromesh and traditional lattice-work and burlap arrangements to fabric planting bags.

PLANTING IN A BASKET

1 *Prepared soil or aquatic planting compost is put into the basket. Those with wide mesh sides should be lined with burlap to prevent soil spillage.*

2 *Prepare the plant by removing at least three-quarters of the foliage. Shorten back the root growth. A plant which is disturbed during its growing season dies back anyway, so removing excess growth works to its advantage and ensures rapid re-establishment.*

3 *For marginal aquatics multiple plantings are to be prepared. Allow three or four plants for each basket. Firm the plants in well and top up with compost as necessary. An initial watering settles the compost and drives out any air.*

Above: *Congested plantings of marginal and bog garden plants like irises require regular dividing and replanting.*

4 Top off the planting with a generous layer of well-washed pea gravel. This prevents soil spillage and fish disturbance.

5 With planting complete, surplus burlap from the lining of the basket should be trimmed off neatly with a pair of scissors.

6 The completed planting should be thoroughly watered before being placed in position in the pond. This drives out all the air and settles the compost.

natural planting

There are occasions when planting directly into the pool is desirable. This is mostly when the pool has a natural soil bottom, or alternatively there is a liner sandwiched between the excavated shape and a generous layer of soil. In both cases the control of the spread of the plants has to be by soil sculpting. This is the varying of the internal levels of the pool so that only plants of certain kinds can grow. For example, if there is a shallow area of water 6 in. (15 cm) deep where typha is flourishing, and the pool profile suddenly drops to 2 ft. (60 cm), the typha becomes restricted as it cannot survive in a 2 ft. (60 cm) depth of water. Thus the edge of the planting and its ultimate shape can be determined by the line of excavation between the 6 in. (15 cm) and 2 ft. (60 cm) depths. The growth of the typha follows the area where the depth falls away.

It is quite possible to push bare-rooted plants into the mud on the floor of a naturally lined pool and for them to quickly establish. However, a much better start is achieved if initial plantings are made with an aquatic planting compost or prepared soil, the plants being wrapped in a textile which slowly deteriorates, but from which their roots can escape.

PLANTING A SOIL ROLL

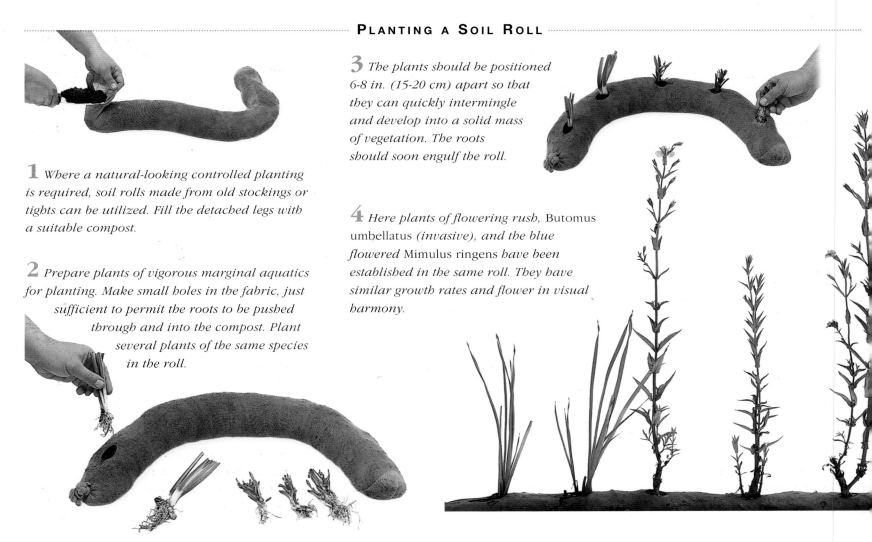

1 *Where a natural-looking controlled planting is required, soil rolls made from old stockings or tights can be utilized. Fill the detached legs with a suitable compost.*

2 *Prepare plants of vigorous marginal aquatics for planting. Make small holes in the fabric, just sufficient to permit the roots to be pushed through and into the compost. Plant several plants of the same species in the roll.*

3 *The plants should be positioned 6-8 in. (15-20 cm) apart so that they can quickly intermingle and develop into a solid mass of vegetation. The roots should soon engulf the roll.*

4 *Here plants of flowering rush,* Butomus umbellatus *(invasive), and the blue flowered* Mimulus ringens *have been established in the same roll. They have similar growth rates and flower in visual harmony.*

Above: *Reeds such as typhas are much loved residents of the wildlife pond and require thoughtful planting if their naturally invasive behavior is to be controlled without stunting their growth.*

1 *Planting in an earth-bottomed pool can be assisted by the use of burlap wraps. Take a bare-rooted plant, add aquatic planting compost and place on a burlap square.*

2 *Wrap the rootball up, securing it like a small parcel. Soak it thoroughly in water to drive out the air before lowering it into its permanent position in the pond.*

3 *Plants planted in burlap wraps are a perfect solution for the earth-bottomed pool. The roots penetrate the burlap and establish quickly into surrounding soil. Within a couple of seasons the burlap rots away without having impaired the development of the plants.*

planting a waterlily

Waterlilies are not only the most decorative and important aquatic plants, but also the longest-lived and most expensive acquisitions for the pool. When purchasing a waterlily the cost is likely to be as much as a young decorative garden tree and the prospect of longevity much the same, although a waterlily does require regularly dividing.

The growth of every plant reflects the soil in which it is growing and for waterlilies this is particularly true, for they are gross feeders. This demand for nutrients used to be met by the liberal use of well-rotted manure or decomposing turf and many old gardening books made this recommendation. The problem with this was that

although the waterlilies prospered, so too did the various slimes and algaes which discolor pond water. The pool was a permanent nutrient-rich environment over which the gardener had no control.

Waterlilies are now widely sold growing in containers and often these can be introduced directly to the pool where they will grow away for a season without requiring any attention. Even if they require immediate repotting, container-grown waterlilies are still the best option for the newcomer to water gardening; and with a balanced planting compost the requirements of the plants and the continued clarity of the water are both addressed.

PREPARING AND PLANTING A WATERLILY

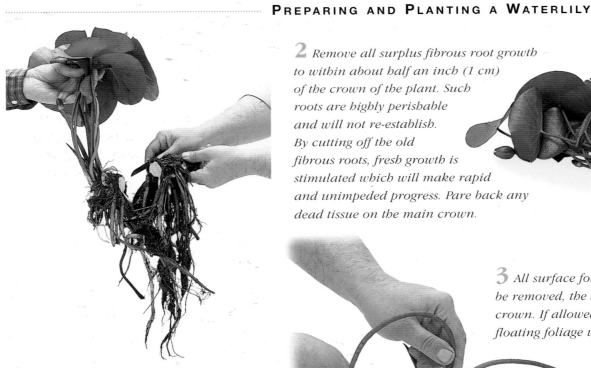

1 *Select a strong-growing crown from a clump of waterlilies and remove any old or dying root system. As most waterlilies grow, they push out new creeping root systems, and the starchy remains of the old are of no further value.*

2 *Remove all surplus fibrous root growth to within about half an inch (1 cm) of the crown of the plant. Such roots are highly perishable and will not re-establish. By cutting off the old fibrous roots, fresh growth is stimulated which will make rapid and unimpeded progress. Pare back any dead tissue on the main crown.*

3 *All surface foliage and developing flower buds should be removed, the stems being cut back close to the main crown. If allowed to remain, the majority of surface floating foliage will in any event become yellow and die. In the meantime it can serve as an undesirable buoyancy aid and lift the plant out of its basket.*

4 *The ideal waterlily crown should consist of a solid portion of starchy root system with a strong growing point with vigorous spear-like underwater shoots. Embryo flower buds can remain, as these may develop into blossoms in favorable growing conditions.*

5 Prepare a large planting basket with a suitable growing medium and plant the waterlily firmly in the center. Water the compost to drive out the air.

6 Top-dress the container with washed pea gravel to reduce soil spillage and disturbance by fish once it is placed into the pool. Water again thoroughly.

7 Newly planted waterlilies can be placed on the floor of the pool in their final positions. They will rapidly establish themselves, producing a mass of fibrous roots and both submerged and floating foliage. Planted before mid-summer, a reasonable show of flowers can be expected in the first season.

Above: *Waterlilies need periodic lifting, dividing and replanting. The first sign of crowding is when the central group of leaves starts climbing out of the water.*

division of a crowded marginal

Pond plants grow very quickly and marginal aquatics in particular require dividing often if they are to maintain the best quality flowers and foliage. In some cases this is as often as every second season. Division is also necessary with named varieties to guarantee that when propagated they are true to type. Seed-raised individuals from named varieties rarely come true.

Unlike plants in an herbaceous border which can be lifted and divided at any time during the dormant season, aquatic plants have to be divided during the spring. They can also be divided during the summer growing season, but in order for this to be carried out successfully the foliage and root systems have to be quite severely cut back. This then impairs the display, whereas if division takes place just as the plants start into growth, they develop unimpeded and flower satisfactorily that season.

With all aquatic plants it is essential to choose the young vigorous outer growths for replanting. The inner woody portions, although often appearing to be more substantial, rarely have the vigor exhibited by outer growths and generally produce a second-class display.

Right: *Crowded marginal aquatics like these calthas must be regularly divided and replanted to maintain their quality.*

DIVISION AND REPLANTING

1 *Clump-forming marginal pond plants like this double flowered marsh marigold,* Caltha palustris *'Flore Pleno,' must be treated ruthlessly, but carefully. It will create a large number of divisions, each of which will be the same as the adult plant. Only use the very best divisions for replanting.*

2 *Remove all the roots to within 1 inch (about 2-3 cm) of the crown. These are highly perishable and are in any event likely to die back.*

3 *Remove all the adult foliage with a sharp knife. The mature leaves of transplanted aquatics usually collapse and fade. It is best to give the new plant a fresh start.*

4 *Plants such as marsh marigolds will often divide into numerous young plantlets or divisions. Any shoot with a small crown and roots can be planted and will ultimately become a worthwhile specimen. For immediate replanting in the decorative pond, only use the more vigorous and larger young divisions. Make sure that they are of uniform size.*

5 *Use a specially prepared aquatic planting compost or good clean garden soil and fill the container to within about an inch (2-3 cm) of the top. This container is made from a rot-proof fabric and is sufficient to accommodate three plants. When planting make sure that the compost is firm.*

6 *Top-dress the compost with a layer of washed pea gravel and water well to drive out any air from the compost before lowering the container into the pond.*

7 *During the late spring and summer marginal plants which are divided re-establish themselves very quickly, many of the mid- to late summer flowering varieties making a reasonable show the same season. These calthas show the benefit of removing old foliage before division, new growth appearing within three or four weeks of division.*

fertilizing plants

Pond plants by their very nature are vigorous growers and heavy feeders. They require fertilizing at least once every season, but this has to be done in such a way that it benefits the plants and does not leach out into the water where it can encourage the development of a green algal bloom. The requirements of the first season after planting can be overcome by selecting a suitable well-balanced aquatic planting compost. Such a compost should contain sufficient nutrients to allow lusty growth for an entire season with no requirement for feeding until early the following summer. Most specialist-manufactured aquatic planting composts are well formulated and provide the likely nutritional requirements of all aquatic plants.

The pool itself will yield nutrients too, both from the inevitable decomposition of aquatic vegetation as well as the deposits from fish. However, in a well-balanced pool this will be insufficient to sustain the kind of growth and flowering that we expect from decorative pond plants if water clarity is to also be assured. The careful use of selected artificial fertilizers is desirable.

Aquatic plant fertilizer is available in small plastic sachets with perforations which permit the absorption of water. The sachet is pressed into the compost next to each plant.

MAKING BONEMEAL PILLS

1 *Take wet clay and mold it into small balls. Add up to 25 per cent by volume of bonemeal or fishmeal, rolling the material into the ball.*

2 *Place the fertilizer pill into the compost next to the plant. Nutrients will be slowly released into the compost without polluting the water.*

Left: *There are several standard pill-like slow-release fertilizers which can be used for aquatic plants in the same way as for shrubs and border subjects.*

Right: *Pond plants are gross feeders and require regular fertilizing if they are to maintain their quality and vigor. Over-fertilizing encourages the growth of algae.*

FEEDING PLANTS

All aquatic plants require nourishment, but not all demand formal feeding. Both submerged and floating aquatics derive their nutrients directly from the water, in the case of submerged plants their root systems performing an anchoring role rather than one which yields up nutrients. In the main they are foliar feeders and extract nutrients from the water rather than the growing medium. Thus in the well-maintained pond where plants and livestock exist in harmony, all the nourishment required comes from the water, at the same time creating conditions which water-discoloring algae find hard to tolerate.

Above: *When fertilizer leaches into the water, slime and algae become a problem. Keep it contained within the compost adjacent to the roots of the plants.*

Waterlilies, deep-water aquatics and marginal plants on the other hand benefit from regular feeding. These derive their nourishment principally from the growing medium. While this should be enriched for the benefit of the plants, it should be done in such a way that there is minimal leaching into the water. When fertilizer is rapidly soluble or escapes into the water, then a green algal bloom follows which obscures pond life.

planting bog plants

Unlike marginal and deep-water aquatic plants, those of the bog garden must be planted during the traditional planting season, from autumn until late spring. Pot- or container-grown plants can be planted at any time but the best results are obtained from a dormant planting of a bare-rooted plant lifted straight from the nursery.

It is important that bog plants have proper boggy conditions and not just damp ones, so correct provision should be made which ensures that the bog garden does not sit permanently under water, but that the soil is saturated, yet without even occasional surface puddles.

Often a bog garden is contrived as an element next to a pond and is constructed at the same time, the water from the pond seeping through a permeable barrier and maintaining the moisture level of the bog garden at the desired level. This is the ideal, for the conditions in the bog garden can be readily controlled.

Alternatively the bog area can be built alongside the pool with its own water supply. This is less desirable, but in most cases is the only way in which a boggy area can be established adjacent to an already established pool.

Above: *A bog garden or moist streamside provides a home for perennials which cannot be grown in permanent standing water.*

CREATING A BOG AREA

1 *A bog garden can be created as part of a pool at the same time as its construction, or as a separate entity, as here.*

2 *An excavation is lined with pool liner and drainage holes created with a fork.*

3 *The drainage holes help to prevent winter waterlogging as does a generous layer of up to 6 in. (20 cm) of pea gravel. This should be raked out over the floor of the excavation prior to filling the area with soil. The gravel helps to keep the roots of the plants away from standing water.*

4 *Although a bog garden that is created in a lined excavation is likely to be mostly wet, it is possible during dry periods for the lining to have the effect of creating a dry contained area of soil. To combat this, introduce a length of irrigation hose.*

Below: *A small bog garden displaying the diversity of flower and foliage offered by moisture-loving perennials. These consist of irises, hostas, sensitive fern, primulas, mimulus, lobelia and astilbe.*

5 *Add soil and fill the excavation to the top. A richly organic soil is to be preferred. As this is added, position the length of hose, in the lower layer. In dry periods this can be connected to the tap and so will ensure constant moisture. A perforated hose is ideal for this purpose.*

6 *Bog garden plants are ideally planted bare-rooted in the spring just as they are showing signs of growth. Pot-grown specimens can be planted at any time of the year. If the rootball is congested, it should be disrupted at planting time.*

waterlily propagation from eyes

Waterlilies grow from fleshy creeping rootstocks. In a natural pond these spread through the mud on the pool floor and periodically produce fresh clumps of growth from large bud-like crowns. Such growths have developed from eyes. These are dormant buds which appear with varying frequency along the rootstocks of mature waterlilies. Most eyes do not sprout and grow into new plants while part of a long-established root system, but once removed they can quickly be encouraged into growth and will soon become vigorous young plants which in many cases will flower during their second season.

The fleshy part of the rootstock of a waterlily is really a stem with buds, and the removal of dormant buds is akin to taking cuttings. Like the cuttings of other plants, being vegetative they always come completely true to type. The eyes vary in their appearance, but mostly they will have produced a couple of small leaves and perhaps an occasional adventitious root. Varieties derived from *Nymphaea tuberosa* are slightly different. The eyes of these are like rounded lumps or nodules and appear attached to the rootstock, rather than as a part of it. They are quite brittle and easily dislodged.

EYE PROPAGATION

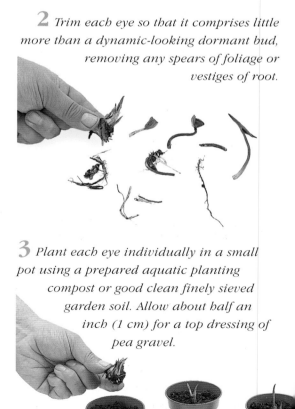

2 Trim each eye so that it comprises little more than a dynamic-looking dormant bud, removing any spears of foliage or vestiges of root.

1 Remove eyes from the rootstock with a sharp knife, with a sliver of starchy tissue attached. The eyes will vary in size and stages of development from dormant buds to young sprouting growths. Each has the capability to develop into a viable plant if handled carefully.

3 Plant each eye individually in a small pot using a prepared aquatic planting compost or good clean finely sieved garden soil. Allow about half an inch (1 cm) for a top dressing of pea gravel.

A mature waterlily has a fleshy rootstock along which are dormant buds or eyes. If removed, these can be rooted and established as young plants.

4 *Place the pots into a bowl of water with the leaves just over the top of the pot. As the eyes break into growth, raise the level slightly to permit the extension of the leaf stalks. Keep the plants in full light and regularly remove any filamentous algae.*

5 *After five or six weeks the plants will start to develop and become recognizable as young waterlilies. Gradually increase the water level in the container and allow the plants to grow on until they fill the small pots with roots. At this stage they are ready to plant out permanently in the garden pond.*

Right: *Although it is possible to raise seedlings from waterlilies like 'Pink Sensation,' the progeny are never true to type and usually inferior. Propagation by eyes guarantees that the young plants are exactly like the parent.*

division propagation – reeds and rushes

The division of aquatic plants is one of the principal and most successful methods of propagation. For the majority of reeds and rushes it is the only method that is likely to work for the home gardener. Some reeds and rushes do produce seed, but its germination is erratic. Its viability is also very dependent upon the season and it can mostly only be obtained by gathering fresh from growing plants. Seed merchants rarely offer such seed. In many cases it does not come true, particularly with mutants like the distinctively marked zebra rush, *Schoenoplectus tabernaemontani* 'Zebrinus.'

Division offers the best solution providing that it is undertaken in the spring just as fresh growth is emerging. Making divisions just as the parent plant is coming into active growth more or less guarantees that the young divisions will grow away strongly once detached.

Among the reeds and rushes are a number of different rootstocks, ranging from the vigorous creeping *Typha latifolia,* with viciously pointed rhizomes as thick as a finger, to the congested clusters of roots and bulbils of the invasive *Butomus umbellatus* and the straightforward fibrous root system of the *Juncus* species. All are easily divisible providing a small growing point is retained.

Many reeds and rushes have very vigorous root systems which are sometimes not contained by a micromesh planting basket. All can be increased by division.

1 *The flowering rush can be readily increased from tiny bulbils which collect around the fleshy creeping rootstock. These are really part of the plant's overwintering mechanism, but when removed are perfect for propagation.*

2 *The bulbils look like large grains of cereal, but are tight buds just waiting to burst into growth. Many have roots present. Plant individually in small pots in a good aquatic planting compost.*

3 *After a couple of months a bulbil will have produced a potful of roots and become well established with extensive leaf development. Once the pot is congested with roots, the young plant can be removed and planted in its permanent position in a planting basket.*

Above: *There is a wide variety of reeds, rushes and aquatic grasses. While some can be increased from seed, all can be propagated by division.*

PROPAGATING RUSHES

1 *Division is the only way to propagate the corkscrew rush and ensure that the twisted characteristic is retained. Take a sharp knife and separate rooted portions.*

2 *As this plant is a mutation, it is important that only divisions which clearly show the corkscrew-type characteristic are retained. The straight stemmed division will revert to the common type if potted up.*

3 *Remove the foliage to within about an inch (2-3 cm) of the crown and similarly trim the roots back hard. Pot individual divisions in pots in a prepared aquatic planting compost. Stand in shallow water.*

division propagation – other marginals

While there are specialist root systems and forms of division, largely among the reeds and rushes, the majority of marginal aquatic plants are lifted and divided in much the same way as their herbaceous border relatives. The main difference is that aquatic plants must be divided during the growing season, between late spring and late summer, whereas those of the border are usually dealt with during the autumn and winter.

For most marginal plants spring division is best, just as the new season's growth is appearing. By doing this, young plants can have a whole growing season before them. Also those that are planted back into the pond for display purposes have the prospect of producing a reasonable show if re-established before the summer.

There are exceptions, notably irises. While these can be successfully lifted and divided in the spring, doing so ruins their early summer display. It is much better to follow tradition and to lift and divide aquatic irises immediately after flowering. Thus the current season's display is assured and the divisions which are placed immediately after flowering are sufficiently well established to make a good display the next summer. Indeed, they are often sizable clumps again at flowering time.

DIVISION OF IRISES

1 *Irises, or other similar marginal plants such as* Acorus, *should be separated into individual fans of leaves and have both roots and foliage trimmed back.*

2 *The individual plant divisions should be potted in aquatic planting compost and stood with water just above the rims of the pots. After six to eight weeks they can be planted out.*

DIVISION OF CLUMP-FORMING MARGINALS

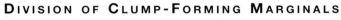

1 *Many marginal plants, such as* Mimulus ringens, *grow in tight clumps and can be lifted periodically and separated into individual plants.*

2 *The foliage should be cut back to within 2-4 in. (5-10 cm) of the base and the roots reduced to about 1 inch. (2-3 cm). Pot individually in small pots containing aquatic planting compost and stand in water which is just above the rims of the pots.*

Above: *Named varieties of marginals like the variegated* Iris *can only be successfully propagated by division.*

DIVIDING DWARF MARGINALS

1 *There are several short-growing plants, like* Sisyrinchium angustifolium, *which produce myriad tiny divisions that require treating like seedlings in a seed tray.*

2 *The individual divisions should have the foliage and roots reduced to about half their length. They should then be pricked out into a seed tray in an aquatic planting compost.*

3 *After a couple of months standing in a tray of shallow water, they develop enough to be potted individually in aquatic planting compost topped with pea gravel.*

stem cuttings

Stem cuttings are a traditional method of increasing a wide array of garden plants. They can equally well be utilized for many aquatic plants, especially marginal and bog garden subjects. As the plants which we grow in our ponds are often very different from those of the herbaceous bed and border, it is often unclear to the newcomer to water gardening as to which can be increased by this method.

Irrespective of the variety, there is a good general rule which can be applied to determine whether a plant will root from a stem cutting. If the plant has leaves with veins in a net arrangement, e.g. *Mimulus*, it can be increased from a cutting. If the leaves have parallel veins, e.g. *Iris*, then stem

cuttings are out. To confirm suitability further check with the flowers. All plants producing blossoms with three, six or multiples of three petals cannot be rooted from stem cuttings; those with four, five or more petals, but which are not divisible by three, can all be increased from cuttings. This is a useful tip in determining the viability of this propagation technique with other garden plants as well.

Of course the plant to be propagated has to produce suitable short stems from which to make cuttings and these should ideally be fresh and healthy with no intention of flowering. With most aquatics such shoots are usually evident during late spring.

CREEPING STEM CUTTINGS

1 *The fact that the bog arum,* Calla palustris, *has a creeping stem does not mean that the opportunities for propagation are limited. The main growing point can be removed and planted individually, the long creeping leafless stem being converted into propagation material.*

2 *Select firm growth and cut sections of stem up to 2 in. (3-5 cm) long, each with a fresh green dormant bud in the center. Remove any stem scales and vestiges of root.*

3 *Pot each stem section horizontally with the bud uppermost in individual pots filled with aquatic compost. Water thoroughly.*

4 *Place the pots into a bowl with the water just over the pot rims. If prior watering was thorough, any escape of air from the compost should not displace the cuttings.*

5 *Cuttings taken during late spring or early summer will have developed into adult plants by late summer.*

TRADITIONAL STEM CUTTINGS

1 *Creeping plants like brooklime,* Veronica beccabunga, *can be easily and quickly increased by short stem cuttings taken from late spring until mid-summer.*

2 *Make short jointed cuttings for preference, always severing them at a leaf joint. This is the part of the stem where the cells that are stimulated into root production are most numerous. Trim the lower leaves and remove any flowers.*

3 *Place the cuttings around the edge of a pot in aquatic planting compost or finely sieved soil and stand in a bowl with water just covering the pot rims.*

4 *After three or four week the cuttings will have rooted and will be well established in the pot. They then start to become crowded and, if not separated out, will grow into a great tangle and thus be spoiled.*

5 *Separate out the plants and pot them individually in an aquatic planting compost. In order to develop bushy growth, the tops of the cuttings should be pinched out at leaf joints. The buds in the angles of all the leaves will then break out and produce fresh shoots. These in turn can be pinched back to encourage a dense habit of growth.*

Above: *The only reliable method of increasing the bog bean,* Menyanthes trifoliata, *is by stem cuttings using the same method as employed for* Calla palustris. *This should be done in early summer after flowering.*

propagating submerged plants

Submerged aquatic plants are for the most part increased from cuttings, although there are a couple of species which are clump-forming and increased by division. These are common hair grass, *Eleocharis acicularis*, and *Isoetes lacustris*, a short-growing rush-like plant which is not widely cultivated. These two are merely divided into separate plantlets and replanted in the same way as marginal subjects. All other submerged aquatics are increased from stem cuttings which are made into bunches fastened together at the base with a short strip of lead.

The cuttings of submerged plants should all be taken from the current season's growth. Propagation can therefore take place at any time from late spring until late summer. Although taking cuttings is a method of increasing plant stock, with many species it is part of a maintenance program, for after a season established clumps look very weary. However, being quick-growing, fresh young stock can be used as replacement each season if cuttings are taken as early in the spring as possible.

Spring growth is always the easiest to propagate. That produced towards the end of the summer will often become brittle and be difficult to bunch, especially growth which has recently flowered.

PROPAGATING A SUBMERGED PLANT

1 *Remove established growth from the pool which has young shoots at least 2 in. (5 cm) long. Wash the vegetation thoroughly and remove any clinging filamentous algae.*

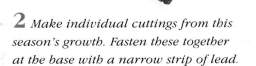

2 *Make individual cuttings from this season's growth. Fasten these together at the base with a narrow strip of lead.*

3 *Insert the bunches of cuttings into a basket of aquatic planting compost. Ensure that the lead around each bunch is buried or it will rot through the stems and the tops of the cuttings will float to the surface.*

4 *Top off the planting with a generous layer of well-washed pea gravel. This helps to prevent soil spillage into the water and deters the fish from disturbing the basket.*

5 *Position the basket in the pool having first watered it thoroughly to drive all the air out of the compost. This prevents violent bubbling and the disturbance of the cuttings.*

6 *After a month, the cuttings will have become well established and a container of lush submerged vegetation will result.*

Above: *Submerged aquatic plants depend upon regular propagation and replacement to remain strong and of vigorous growth. This is essential to maintain a healthy, well-balanced aquatic environment for the fish and other aquatic life to enjoy.*

raising from seed

Many aquatic plants can be successfully raised from seed, although it is wise to check first to see whether any other propagation method is appropriate. Seed raising can produce a considerable number of plants, but it often takes a lot longer for them to become of sufficient size for planting out compared with those grown from cuttings or division.

Seed-raised plants are only of species or strains. For the most part, named varieties of garden plants, whether aquatic or not, do not come true to type from seed. There are occasional exceptions, such as the bog garden primula,

Primula japonica 'Postford White.' That is not to say that good seed-raised strains of aquatics are in any way inferior; indeed among the mimulus the commercial selections are mostly far superior to the named varieties, which have to be increased from cuttings.

Often the seed of aquatic plants has to be gathered from growing plants. Few seed companies stock pond plant seed, as in most cases its viability is limited. The best results are achieved by sowing seeds collected directly from the parent plant immediately after it has ripened.

RAISING AQUATICS FROM SEED

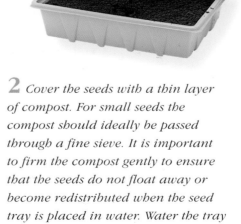

1 *True aquatic plants can often be raised from seed, but almost without exception this must be freshly gathered on the point of ripening and sown immediately. Bog garden seeds are more conventional and some, like mimulus and primula, are available commercially and are sown in early spring. Use a good seed compost and distribute the seed sparingly over the surface of the seed tray.*

2 *Cover the seeds with a thin layer of compost. For small seeds the compost should ideally be passed through a fine sieve. It is important to firm the compost gently to ensure that the seeds do not float away or become redistributed when the seed tray is placed in water. Water the tray gently from above before placing it in standing water so that any air in the compost is driven out.*

3 *Bog garden seeds like mimulus should be subjected to wet conditions, but must not be submerged. Place the seed tray in a deeper tray with sufficient water so that the level outside is equivalent to the surface level of the compost within the tray. An excess of water will rot the seeds.*

Right: *Most species and mixed strains of bog garden plants can be raised successfully from seed, including candelabra primulas like the crimson flowered* Primula japonica.

4 *When the seedlings have germinated and the first rough leaves are showing, they should be separated and pricked out into a seed tray to grow on.*

5 *Once the seed tray becomes full of roots and the foliage is a congested mass, the young plants can be lifted carefully and either potted individually or planted directly outside.*

root cuttings and plantlets

It often surprises gardeners that many herbaceous plants can be increased quickly and successfully from root cuttings and plantlets. Among the plants that we popularly grow in our water gardens, it is the bog garden subjects that are most amenable to this form of propagation. Primulas are particularly agreeable to root-cutting propagation, so too *Houttuynia*, although this spreads so quickly that plantlet divisions are a better option when only a few plants are required. As with stem cuttings, the propagation of plants from root cuttings and division guarantees that the progeny are true to type.

The principle which permits root cuttings to be successful is similar to that of suckering. Many plants have roots which have latent buds that remain dormant until the root is damaged, typically seen as suckering. By removing pieces of root from plants which have dormant buds, the buds are stimulated into growth.

***Right:** Candelabra primulas are excellent plants to increase from either root cuttings or plantlets. Root cuttings are usually taken during the winter, while root divisions are made immediately after flowering during summer.*

TAKING ROOT CUTTINGS

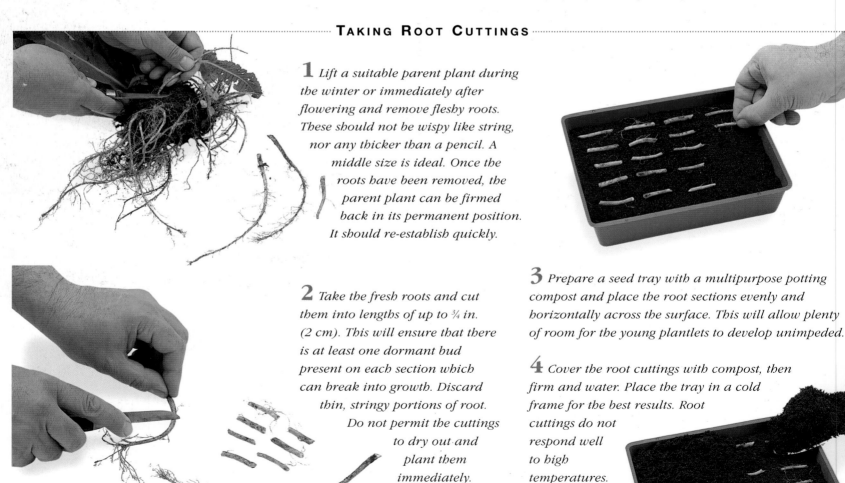

1 *Lift a suitable parent plant during the winter or immediately after flowering and remove fleshy roots. These should not be wispy like string, nor any thicker than a pencil. A middle size is ideal. Once the roots have been removed, the parent plant can be firmed back in its permanent position. It should re-establish quickly.*

2 *Take the fresh roots and cut them into lengths of up to ¾ in. (2 cm). This will ensure that there is at least one dormant bud present on each section which can break into growth. Discard thin, stringy portions of root. Do not permit the cuttings to dry out and plant them immediately.*

3 *Prepare a seed tray with a multipurpose potting compost and place the root sections evenly and horizontally across the surface. This will allow plenty of room for the young plantlets to develop unimpeded.*

4 *Cover the root cuttings with compost, then firm and water. Place the tray in a cold frame for the best results. Root cuttings do not respond well to high temperatures.*

SEPARATING PLANTLETS

1 *Some bog garden plants, such as primulas, can be lifted straight after flowering, have their foliage cut hard back and then be divided.*

2 *Separate out the tiniest individuals. These will eventually make new plants. Trim back the roots and pot the small divisions individually in potting compost. Plant the larger divisions directly outdoors.*

storing plants overwinter

The majority of hardy aquatic plants survive the winter without any difficulty. However, there are benefits to be obtained through making some provisions for storage of their winter growth in order that young plants can have a head start in the spring. This particularly applies to floating aquatics.

Most floating species produce winter buds or turions and if these can be afforded some winter protection, they can be started into growth much earlier in the spring. Under natural conditions turions fall to the bottom of the pool at the approach of autumn. Here they remain until the spring sun warms up the water, when they return to the surface and grow out into new plants. In some instances, such as frogbit, *Hydrocharis morsus-ranae*, the winter stage is a tight bud reminiscent of a bulbil; with others, seeds are produced. In the pool it would be impossible to gather these to start into growth, but by overwintering them in a container with some water, early development can be assured if a little warmth is applied.

Other turions benefit from protection from winter predators, among them the sagittarias or arrowheads. These plants produce small turions like potatoes, which are much-loved by wild fowl.

OVERWINTERING WATER HYACINTH

2 *The water hyacinth does not overwinter well in deep water. It much prefers to remain in a shallow bowl in a muddy gruel. The bottom of the bowl should be covered with a generous layer of aquatic planting compost into which the plant can root if it desires. Keep in full light at a minimum temperature of 50°F (10°C).*

1 *Water hyacinth,* Eichhornia crassipes, *is not hardy in areas subject to frost. Select young vigorous plantlets for overwintering indoors. Discard old plants.*

Ceratophyllum demersum *or hornwort produces small brush-like winter buds. Place a few of these in a jar of water with soil on the bottom and keep in the light so as to get some early growth.*

OVERWINTERING FAIRY MOSS

1 *Fairy moss,* Azolla filiculoides, *is a floating aquatic which is not reliably hardy. It often disappears for the winter and reappears during the late spring.*

2 *To ensure its survival and to guarantee some healthy growth early in the spring, it can be easily overwintered by being placed in a container of water with a layer of soil on the bottom in early autumn.*

3 *The container should be positioned in a well-lit place and kept at a minimum temperature of 41°F (5°C). Remove any mold that may occasionally develop.*

STORING TURIONS

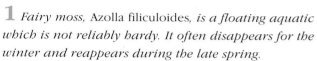

1 *All arrowheads,* Sagittaria, *produce turions. These are vulnerable to wildlife, especially wild fowl. Arrowheads also benefit from kick-starting into early spring growth with a little protection. Turions can be removed from a mature plant in late summer.*

2 *Turions are highly perishable and should be stored in damp sand during the winter. Place them in layers in a jar and store in a cool frost-free place. They are removed in early spring and planted in pots until sprouting vigorously, when they can be planted out permanently.*

OVERWINTERING WATER LETTUCE

1 *Water lettuce,* Pistia stratiotes, *is an attractive tropical floating plant which spends the summer outdoors in the pool. It starts to suffer when the temperature drops below 50°F (10°C). The older plants are difficult to overwinter, so select vigorous young plantlets which are still attached to the parent and bring them indoors in early autumn.*

2 *Water lettuce is difficult to overwinter in deep water. It requires a bowl of water with a layer of soil on the bottom, plenty of light and a temperature of 64°F (18°C).*

care and maintenance

Like all garden features a water garden demands regular care and attention. However, a great deal can be done to ensure that this is as simple as possible by planning carefully from the beginning. If the compost is suitably prepared so that the plants are content, and there is little opportunity for leaching of nutrients into the water, then problems with green water will be minimized provided that sufficient plants are introduced. Creating and maintaining a balance among floating plants, deep-water aquatics with floating foliage and submerged plants is the key to a successful pond.

Fish also make a contribution, but they are mainly decorative, the clearing up of aquatic insect pests and mosquito larvae being their principal benefit. Ramshorn snails graze on filamentous algae, while freshwater mussels act as living filters and remove suspended algae from the water.

Routine care is mainly confined to the spring and summer months, the regular dividing and manicuring of plants being necessary to maintain their vigor. Fertilizing is also essential using specially prepared sachets or tablets that will not pollute the water. During winter all the plants become dormant and require no attention, although the fish must be taken care of when the temperature drops below freezing. It is essential that ice is not permitted to cover the water surface and trap noxious gases beneath it which may asphyxiate the fish.

During the summer it is not essential to feed the fish unless there is an over-population in terms of a naturally achieved balance. When fishkeeping is the dominant influence in the water garden, regular feeding is important and water filtration essential.

A well-maintained garden pond is truly a thing of beauty.

pond chemistry

Understanding the chemistry of the pond is important if a good quality of water is to be maintained. If there is no overstocking of fish and plants are installed in numbers and varieties that ensure a natural balance, then there are few problems. However, it is as well to be aware of what can go wrong and why.

Problems mostly occur if the plant population goes into decline and fish population levels rise. This can have an adverse effect upon the nitrogen cycle. It is the lack of control of nitrogenous wastes deriving from the fish that can lead to problems, especially a rise in ammonia levels.

In nature nitrifying bacteria break down toxic wastes into less harmful products. This takes place as part of what is known as the nitrogen cycle. Organic material usually contains proteins in variable amounts. When protein is broken down either by bacterial decomposition or as a waste product of protein metabolism, ammonia is formed. Bacterial action converts ammonia, which is extremely toxic to fish, into less toxic nitrites. These in turn are converted into nitrates which are relatively harmless substances which are taken up as 'food' by plants and used in the construction of plant proteins. The process of converting ammonia into nitrate is called nitrification.

When there are considerable numbers of fish, this process, which naturally occurs in the pond, will benefit from the action of a biological filter. Such a filter provides a home for beneficial bacteria to prosper. Even when the water chemistry of a pond appears to be healthy, it is wise to check periodically for nitrites. Most garden centres offer simple test kits which can be easily used by the gardener.

The digestive processes of fish break down plant proteins and create ammonia as one of the waste by-products.

Plants absorb nitrates, which are used to produce proteins.

Aerobic bacteria oxidize and convert nitrite into nitrate.

Ammonia is toxic and present both in fish excretions and decaying food and plant material.

Aerobic bacteria oxidize harmful ammonia converting it into less toxic nitrites.

The Nitrogen Cycle *This is how nitrogen circulates in a pond. The bacteria that convert one nitrogen-containing compound into another occur naturally. It is essential to encourage them to thrive in filters to prevent ammonia and nitrite building up.*

They involve mixing a small sample of pond water with a chemical which then turns colour and is compared with a test chart. There is a similar test which can determine the relative acidity or pH of the water. Although this is rarely as critical as for nitrite, it is useful to keep an eye on the acidity of the water.

While a natural balance of plants and sensible stocking level with fish is the most satisfactory method of maintaining stability, the introduction of physical, biological and UV filters can be recommended, depending upon circumstances. Using an air pump to improve the oxygen content of the water is also invaluable, especially where there is a heavy population of fish. These resemble aquarium pumps and they can improve water quality considerably, especially in the murky, often lifeless, bottom of the deeper pool.

TESTING POND WATER

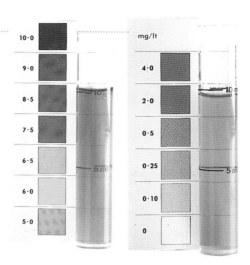

1 The testing of pond water should be carried out routinely. It is essential to obtain a typical fresh sample in a small test tube.

2 For a pH test for water acidity a tablet is dissolved in the water sample. This colors the water, which is then matched against a chart.

3 The results of most pond water tests are analyzed against a graduated color chart of comparative readings. The sample on the left shows a broad-range pH reading, while that on the right gives the result of a simple test for nitrite levels in the pond water.

Above: An air pump dissipates oxygen through the water. This is helpful to fish and improves water quality.

Above: A UV filter is extremely valuable for the control of algae suspended in the water.

Above: A very healthy, well-planted and carefully maintained pond demonstrating how good water quality can benefit its inhabitants. The water has a clear reflective appearance which indicates that it is well oxygenated and in excellent condition.

stocking a pond with fish

No natural pond would be complete without its complement of fish. Apart from bringing life to the water, they help to control undesirable aquatic insect life such as mosquito and gnat larvae. They also feed on Daphnia, caddisflies and other forms of aquatic life that in the more natural pond are regarded as a bonus. In the garden pond caddisflies are a pest, since they strip the foliage of aquatic plants. Conversely in the wildlife pond they are a fascination, for each constructs itself a shelter in which to live out of plant debris and stones. Different species each build a unique kind of shelter.

While fish are useful, it depends upon personal aspirations as to how many are introduced and of which species. Goldfish are extremely useful and resilient. So too their fancy variety, the shubunkin, and the comet-tailed forms of each. Varieties of koi are becoming increasingly popular. Golden orfe are attractive fish which tend to shoal and live towards the surface of the pond.

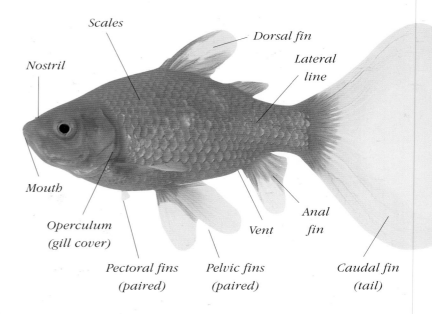

Scales *Dorsal fin* *Lateral line* *Nostril* *Mouth* *Operculum (gill cover)* *Vent* *Anal fin* *Pectoral fins (paired)* *Pelvic fins (paired)* *Caudal fin (tail)*

Before fish are introduced to a pool it is wise to disinfect them. Use a product based upon methylene blue and immerse them in it before returning them to a small bag

INTRODUCING FISH TO A POOL

1 *Prepare fish before introducing them to the pool by equalizing the water temperature in their bag with that in the pool. Roll down the top of the bag to make a collar.*

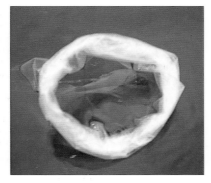

2 *Float the bag containing some of the original water in which the fish were purchased on the surface of the pool . The temperatures will begin to equalize after several minutes.*

3 *Pour some pond water into the bag to assist with the temperature equalization process and to adjust the relative pH levels. Leave the bag for a further 20 minutes or so.*

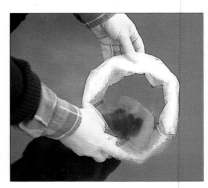

4 *Once the temperature has equalized within the bag, the fish can be gently poured into the pool. For the first few days after introduction they may not be very visible.*

Above: Nishiki koi are very popular fish and are much prized by pond keepers. Unlike goldfish, koi are quite boisterous.

Above: When freshly purchased fish are introduced to a pond, it is prudent to disinfect them with an anti-fungal and anti-bacterial solution. This ensures that they do not bring infection to your pond.

STOCKING LEVELS

Check with a reputable supplier for guidelines on the maximum stocking level for your pond. One rule of thumbe is 1 to 2 square feet of surface area per inch (2.5 cm) of fish. However many fish the pond will theoretically hold, always understock to allow the fish to grow to the natural stocking level of the pond. Overcrowding results in poor growth and outbreaks of disease.

If you are stocking a new pond, allow some days to elapse after filling it with water before you introduce fish. This allows the water chemistry to settle and the filter time to get working, and gives plants the opportunity to establish themselves.

Flakes

Floating sticks

Sinking pellets

Wheatgerm sticks

Left: There are a wide range of fish foods available to the pond keeper, all of which are scientifically produced. It is not really necessary to feed decorative fish in a well-balanced pond, but most water gardeners enjoy doing so.

of water and floating this on the surface of the pond. After a short time, when the temperature of the water inside the bag has equalized with that in the pond, release them into the water as illustrated on the opposite page.

Fish do not have to be fed in a pool that is well stocked with plants and where there is a balanced population. However, few people can resist the temptation of feeding and this can become a regular summer ritual. There are many good foods around including, flakes, pellets and meal.

coping with physical problems

Water features have problems from time to time, irrespective of how carefully they are constructed and maintained. The worst possible problem is a leak. Not that leaks are difficult to repair, since there are repair kits for most water gardening systems. It is finding the leak that causes the greatest difficulty.

The water level usually falls to a point level with the leak. By removing a quantity of water to take the level within the pool a couple of inches (a few cm) lower, the source of the problem is often exposed.

1 *Periodically a beach requires cleaning. Dirt gets between the stones and areas that are constantly wet gather algae.*

2 *Remove all the stones and wash them thoroughly by hand. Hose down the beach area and then replace the stones.*

REPAIRING TORN LINER

Backing tape

Self-adhesive repair tape

Original liner

The first sign of a problem is usually when the water drops to the same level after the pool has been filled several times. If a leak is suspected, lower the water an inch or two (a few cm) and the tear will usually be exposed. Clean the liner thoroughly and allow it to dry. Purchase a suitable repair kit for your liner. There are specific repair kits, rather like those used for mending bicycle tires, for PVC or rubber. Take a suitable size patch to cover the area of the tear completely, press it down firmly and buff it down to secure the seal. Allow it to dry thoroughly before refilling the pool with water.

Fiberglass preformed pools are not so widely used now, but in the past they were among the most popular forms of pool construction. Many have been in the ground for a number of years. Following routine maintenance, when the gardener has often stood in the pool, a crack will appear. It is rarely severe damage, but sufficient to cause irritating seepage. If properly cleaned and dried, this is easily repaired with a do-it-yourself car body repair kit.

There are specific pool repair kits for rigid plastic and preformed pools, while kits that resemble those for repairing punctures are commonly available for rubber, LDPE and PVC pool liners. Take care to obtain the correct kit for the liner and then clean the damaged area thoroughly. Dry it off and apply the patch. Concrete ponds also suffer from leaks. While many fewer are constructed now than previously, there are large numbers still providing gardeners with pleasure. When repairing a concrete leak, it is important to chisel out around the damaged area and to replace with quick-drying cement. Once the cement has dried properly it can be painted over with a pond sealant.

Above: A well-planted pool where the marginal planting has secured the edges from erosion. The water quality is good and everything looks healthy, although the waterlilies are going to require lifting and dividing next spring. The rising foliage of waterlilies above the surface of the water is a sign that they are becoming too crowded.

With natural water features erosion can be a problem, especially when the pond is of natural construction. Larger pools can suffer from wave erosion and even small domestic streams show signs of sheet erosion. This is when water is forced to pass around corners too quickly and bounces from one side of the stream to the other. Planting usually overcomes these problems, densely rooting marginal aquatics like *Mentha aquatica* and *Veronica beccabunga* being ideal to bind the soil together.

Pumps and filters rarely cause problems. Pumps should be regularly inspected and any debris removed. When necessary filters must be cleaned and filter materials replaced. If there is a fault with the pump and it does not function properly after usual routine maintenance has taken place, then discard it, since modern submersible pumps are far better and more safely replaced than having repairs done to them.

Right: A pump must be cleaned regularly. Filamentous algae clings to most objects in a pool if given the opportunity. This greatly impairs its efficiency.

eco-balance and seasonal care

The eco-balance of a water feature once established has to be maintained. It is important to ensure that the balance of submerged subjects and both floating plants and the foliage of deep-water aquatics are controlled satisfactory. Marginal plants, although of no great significance in maintaining a balanced eco-system, can disrupt it considerably if allowed to spread indiscriminately. So the regular lifting, division and trimming of plants is essential both during the spring and into the summer.

Algal growth presents a problem for every pool owner at some time, even if it is only during the first few weeks of early spring when the water has warmed up and the submerged plants are not actively growing and competing with them for mineral salts. Aquatic algae appear in many forms, but there are two main kinds: the free-floating and filamentous. The free-floating kinds are those that occur in great masses and give the water an appearance of pea

soup. The filamentous kinds appear as thick masses of silkweed or blanketweed. There are other species like mermaid's hair that cling to the sides of the pond and to containers, but they enhance rather than detract from the natural water garden.

The best solution for algal problems is to create a natural balance with plants providing competition with algae for nutrients, and surface foliage shading out suspended algae. Chemical controls work, but are only temporary solutions. However, they can be very useful early in the life of the pool while the main plants that are to provide the balance become established. When algaecides are used to kill filamentous algae, then the dead algae must be removed so that it does not deoxygenate the water.

Leaves are also a great problem for pond owners. Natural ponds visually can tolerate a few more than more formal arrangements, but not when it comes to an accumulation

REGULAR MAINTENANCE

Below: *Fallen leaves are a nuisance in a pond, especially at autumn leaf fall. They rapidly sink to the bottom where they slowly decompose and pollute the water. Netting over the pond, or erecting a temporary fence around it to prevent leaves from blowing in is the best preventative. During the summer fallen leaves should be netted out by hand.*

Above: *The occurrence of slime and algae cannot be avoided, even in the best-balanced pools. Throughout the summer it is necessary regularly to remove filamentous algae with a net by hand or by twisting it around a cane. Algaecides can be used but dead algae still has to be removed or it decomposes and deoxygenates the water.*

Above: *As winter approaches it is important to clean up the waterside. Any dead or decaying foliage on marginal or moisture-loving plants should be removed. Faded foliage should be cut back to the ground, but marginals, especially hollow-stemmed species, must not be cut below the water level or else they may rot.*

SEASONAL MAINTENANCE

Spring

- Aquatic plants can be planted.
- Lift and divide waterlilies and marginal plants as necessary.
- Take cuttings from submerged aquatics and replant where necessary.
- Sow the seeds of aquatic plants and bog garden subjects that are available from seed companies.
- Take stem cuttings of selected marginal aquatics. Increase waterlilies from eyes.
- Repot and replace the compost of any plants that require attention, but do not need dividing.
- If the pond requires cleaning out, the spring is the best time to do so.

Summer

- Control filamentous algae by twisting out with a stick.
- Introduce or replace any plants as required.
- Remove faded blossoms from marginal plants.
- Remove surplus carpeting floating plants with a net.
- Fertilize the compost of established waterlilies and marginals.
- Sow freshly collected seeds of aquatic plants.
- Cut back any excessive growth of aquatic plants.

Autumn

- Collect and store plantlets and turions of appropriate aquatics ready for the winter.
- Net the pool to keep out leaves.
- Cut back faded marginal plants, but do not cut hollow-stemmed aquatics below water level or else they might rot.
- Take root cuttings of bog garden plants like primulas.

Winter

- Ensure that an area of the surface is kept free from ice to permit the escape of noxious gases that may harm fish.
- Spray trees of the plum and cherry family with a winter wash to kill off the overwintering generation of waterlily aphids.

causing problems. Irrespective of whether there are trees in your garden, leaves will find their way in during the autumn. They can blow in from neighboring gardens and always tend to swirl around and be pulled down immediately after they come into contact with water.

Some leaves are extremely toxic, not to plants, but to fish and should be excluded by whatever means possible. These include those of the horse chestnut family (*Aesculus*), which are particularly noxious, as well as willows (*Salix*), which have properties similar to aspirin and can harm fish when they decompose in the pool.

The temporary use of netting to protect the pool from fallen leaves is the best way of keeping them out. Covering the pool completely is often recommended, but this is both unsightly and can damage the marginal plants. It is more satisfactory to use small mesh netting about 18 in.

Above: *During winter, spray dormant plum and cherry trees with a winter wash. These are the overwintering host of the troublesome waterlily aphid. Killing the eggs at this stage breaks the life cycle.*

(45 cm) high and to fasten this to stakes around the pool. This prevents the majority of leaves from entering the water as the greater number blow into the pool from the surrounding garden, rather than fall directly from the trees into the water. Small quantities can be scooped out.

During the winter it is important to winter-wash fruit trees of the plum and cherry (*Prunus*) family, for these are the overwintering host of one of the most troublesome aquatic pests, the waterlily aphid. During the autumn adult female aphids migrate to the trees and deposit eggs and die. These can be killed during the winter by spraying with tar oil wash, thus weakening their life cycle. The control of waterlily aphids in the pool, other than by washing off with clear water, is impossible.

maintaining hygiene and winter care

Apart from keeping the water free from algae, water garden maintenance should focus on general hygiene and cleanliness. Detritus and debris should be removed from the pond or water feature. Nowadays this is relatively simple using an aqua vacuum cleaner. This sucks up debris and is very efficient if used regularly and no great accumulation of detritus is allowed to build up.

Leaves can also be a problem, not only those that fall into the pond in the autumn, but those of associated aquatic plants if all-round hygiene is not up to standard. In autumn it is a wise precaution to net the pool before leaf fall. Most leaves blow in from surrounding ground rather than fall directly into the water from above, so a temporary low fence around the water feature is most effective. Install this when the leaves first change color. Such a fence precludes interference with aquatic plants. Leaves that fall directly into the water or accumulate in cascade bowls or waterfall units should also be regularly removed.

As winter approaches tidy up any waterside plants and replace the pump with a pool heater if there are fish. While ornamental pond fish are very hardy, they do run the risk of asphyxiation if the pond freezes over for a period of time. The problem is that the accumulation of organic debris on the floor of the pond or basin produces gases which normally dissipate harmlessly into the atmosphere, but if they become trapped beneath a layer of ice they can cause the fish to suffocate. An alternative to installing a pool heater to keep an area of the pool ice-free is regularly to stand a pan full of boiling water on the ice and permit it to melt through. This creates a hole in the ice through which gases can permeate. Never break the ice as the shock waves traveling through the water may concuss or kill the fish.

Right: This pond feature embraces all that is wonderful about water gardening. Beautifully created moving water in a natural setting is accompanied by a wonderful range of aquatic and bog plants.

WINTER CARE

It is quite natural for leaves to be found lying on the bottom of pool. For most of the year, they decompose slowly and the gases resulting from their decomposition escape into the air. When the pool ices over, they become trapped and can asphyxiate the fish.

From autumn until early spring it is important to remove leaf debris from anywhere in and around the pool. Often dead leaves collect in the waterfall once the water has been switched off for the winter. These can easily blow into the pool.

It is important to create a permanent ice-free area to allow the noxious gases produced by the decomposition of organic matter on the pool floor to escape. A pan of hot water set on the ice and allowed to melt through is a good way of doing this.

index

Picture Credits

Eric Crichton: 13, 27, 28, 31, 33 top, 42, 43 top, 51 (design: Sparsholt College, RHS Chelsea 1997), 53, 57 lower, 61 (Wyevale Garden Centres, RHS Chelsea 2001), 63 (Mrs Daphne Foulsham), 65 (*Country Living* Garden, RHS Chelsea 1993), 67 (RHS Chelsea 1993), 85 lower (Mr and Mrs D. Edwards, Essex/NGS), 86 (Mrs U.Carr, Avon/NGS), 88 left (Simon and Kate Harman, RHS Hampton Court 1999), 90-91 (design: Carol Klein, RHS Chelsea 1999), 95 (Mr and Mrs J. Draper, Denbigh and Colwyn/NGS), 101 left, 106-107 (RHS Chelsea 1998), 107 lower (Mr and Mrs Porteous, Dorset/NGS), 114 (design: Douglas Knight, RHS Chelsea 1993), 115 (Honda Japanese Tea Garden, RHS Chelsea 1995), 117 left, 122, 127 right, 131 left (Barrington Court kitchen garden, National Trust), 137 (design: Alan Sargent, RHS Chelsea 2000), 138, 144-145 (design: S. Rendell and J. Tavender, Dorset Water Lily Co, RHS Hampton Court 2001), 145 (RHS Chelsea 1997), 147 (design: S. Rendell and J. Tavender, Dorset Water Lily Co, RHS Hampton Court 2001), 156-157 (Wyevale Garden Centres, RHS Chelsea 1997), 166 (Mitsubishi Garden, RHS Hampton Court 2001), 171 (design: Arabella Lennox-Boyd, *Evening Standard*, RHS Chelsea 2000), 172 (design: Mamey Hall, RHS Hampton Court 2001), 173 left, 175 (*Country Living* Garden, RHS Chelsea 1993), 180-181 (design: Crockett and Summers, Dorset Water Lily Co, RHS Hampton Court 1999), 184 (design Charles Funk, *Evening Standard*, RHS Chelsea 2001), 190, 193 lower, 197, 203, 204-205, 205, 222, 247 (Lady Johnson, Kent/NGS), 251 (Quarryman's Garden, RHS Chelsea 1998).

John Glover: 2-3, 3, 4, 7, 8-9 (design: Dowle/Gordon, RHS Chelsea 1996), 20-21 (design: Nathalie Charles, RHS Chelsea 2002), 23 right (design: Alan Titchmarsh), 33 lower, 35 (design: Michael Miller, RHS Chelsea 1998), 36, 38, 41, 50 (design: Roger Platts, RHS Chelsea 1996), 54-55, 56, 57 top, 59 (design: Susy Smith), 64, 69 (design: Susy Smith), 75 (design: Hiroshi Nanamori), 81 (design: Mark Walker, RHS Chelsea 1995), 82-83, 84-85, 85 top, 87, 98, 101 right, 112-113 (RHS Chelsea 1996), 121, 123 right, 142-143 (design: Aylesbury College, RHS Chelsea 2002), 157 lower, 169, 181 top, 186-187, 188, 189 left, 189 right, 191 left, 194 left, 194 right, 199, 201, 207, 209 (design: Jane Sweetser, RHS Hampton Court 1999), 210-211, 217, 219, 221, 225, 227 (design: Paul Dyer, RHS Chelsea 1999), 229, 235, 237, 240-241 (design: Roy Day/Steve Hickling, World of Koi, RHS Chelsea 2002).

Jerry Harpur: 157 top (design: David Stevens, RHS Chelsea 1993), 179 (Susanna Brown and Catalyst TV).

Marcus Harpur: 151 left (London Borough of Barnet, RHS Chelsea 2001), 176 (design: Paul Dyer, RHS Hampton Court 2001).

S. and O. Mathews: 88 right, 96-97, 97 top, 97 lower, 105, 107 top, 111 left, 111 right, 116, 127 left, 158, 166-167, 173 right, 191 right, 192, 195, 202, 206 left, 206 right, 231, 233, 245.

Peter McHoy: 24, 117 right.

Clive Nichols Garden Pictures: 15 (Garden and Security Lighting), 22 (design: Andrew and Karla Newell), 23 left (design: Dennis Fairweather), 29 (design: Roger Platts, RHS Chelsea 1996), 32-3 (*Daily Mirror* Garden, RHS Chelsea 1996), 38-39 (design Boardman Gelly & Co, RHS Hampton Court 2000), 39, 49 top, 58 (design: James van Sweden), 58-59 (design: Claus Scheinert), 68 (design: Christian Wright), 71 (Gordon White, Texas), 74 (Spidergarden.com, RHS Chelsea 2000), 76 (design: Shelia Stedman), 76-77 (Tintinhull Gardens, Somerset), 124 (design: Ulf Nordfjell), 133 (design: Alan Sargent, RHS Chelsea 1997), 134-135 (Arrow Cottage, Herefordshire), 139 (design: Myles Challis, RHS Chelsea 1999), 150 (Garden and Security Lighting), 151 right (Garden and Security Lighting), 153 (Garden and Security Lighting), 155 (Garden and Security Lighting), 160, 163 (Architectural Plants, Sussex), 164 (Little Coopers, Hampshire), 178, 181 lower (Brook Cottage, Oxon), 183 (Mr Fraser, design: Julian Treyer-Evans), 185 (design: Ann Firth), 243 (Carolyn Hubble).

Plant Pictures World Wide: 213, 215.

Derek St Romaine: 47 lower right.

Neil Sutherland: 19 top, 43 lower, 45, 72 lower, 89, 100, 123 left, 126, 129, 130, 131 right, 144, 148, 161, 167, 193 top, 196 left, 196 right, 198, 200, 204.